ANOTHER TIME, ANOTHER PLACE

JESSIE KESSON (Jessie Grant McDonald) was born in October 1916 in Inverness. Her childhood was spent in Elgin with her mother—she never knew her father—until she was sent to the orphanage at Skene, Aberdeenshire. After leaving Skene school she entered service, and in 1934 moved to a farm with her husband, who was a cottar. She combined a successful writing career with a variety of jobs, from cleaner to artist's model, and was a social worker for nearly twenty years, settling finally in London with her husband.

The early years of her life influenced much of Jessie Kesson's writing. Her work includes the novels *The White Bird Passes* (1958), turned into an award-winning film in 1980, *Glitter of Mica* (1963), *Another Time, Another Place* (1983), which also became a prize-winning film, and the collection of short stories *Where the Apple Ripens* (1985). In addition, she wrote poetry, newspaper features, and plays for radio and television. Jessie Kesson died in 1994.

Other B&W Titles by Jessie Kesson

THE WHITE BIRD PASSES

JESSIE KESSON

ANOTHER TIME, ANOTHER PLACE

B&W PUBLISHING

First published 1983
This edition published 1997
by B&W Publishing Ltd
Edinburgh
Copyright © Jessie Kesson 1983

The right of Jessie Kesson to be identified
as the Author of this Work has been
asserted by her in accordance with the
Copyright, Designs and Patents Act 1988

ISBN 1 873631 71 5

British Library Cataloguing in Publication Data:
A catalogue record for this book is available
from the British Library

Cover illustration:
Detail from *Cecile Walton* (1918)
by Dorothy Johnstone ARSA (1892-1980)
Photograph by kind permission of
The Flemings Collection

The lines from 'Bless 'em All' by Jimmy Hughes and Frank Lake
© 1940 Keith Prowse Music Pub. Co. Ltd are reproduced by
kind permission of EMI Music Publishing Ltd;
and those from 'Moonlight Becomes You' by James Van Heusen
and Johnny Burke © 1942 Famous Music Corp.
by kind permission of Famous Chappell U.K.

Printed by Werner Söderström

To

Avril and Ken

THERE would be no gathering in of the corn today. The rain that had swept across Inveraig blotted out the firth itself. The corn that had stood just yesterday, high and ripe and ready to fall to the binder, bent earthwards now, beneath the driving lash of the wind.

She could, the young woman thought, be standing high in some inland country, not in a sea-girt place at all. But then, she had not yet become accustomed to this alien place in which she now had her being.

'You'll not be needing the bag apron the day, mistress. I'm saying, Mistress Ainslie.' She turned to find the shepherd at her shoulder. 'I was saying, mistress': it still took her unaware to be addressed by her recently acquired married title, still took her time to respond to it, as if those who uttered it spoke to another person, a different person from the one she knew herself to be.

> *If no-one ever marries me*
> *And I don't see why they should*
> *They say that I'm not pretty*
> *And I'm very seldom good*

1

But someone *had* married her, though she hadn't got used to that either. 'If this wind keeps on rising,' the shepherd prophesied, scanning the sky for a break in the hill-locked clouds, 'it might just manage to dry up the corn.'

'Little chance of that.' Finlay, the farm foreman, ambled towards them, his scythe sheltering under the sacking that should have protected his shoulders. 'If my scythe cannot get at the inroads then it's God help the binder. You'll be a wee thing short in your pay poke,' he warned the young woman, 'if the rain keeps dinging like this. *And* you, Kirsty,' he shouted across the dyke to her neighbour. 'Still. That'll give you both time to catch up with your washing.'

'In weather like this,' Kirsty snapped, rising as always to Finlay's bait, 'there's no drying in it, man.'

'Maybe no then, Kirsty,' Finlay conceded, grinning, 'maybe no. By the by,' he turned again to the young woman, 'you're going to have neighbours next door. *That'll* suit you, that'll keep you from getting lonesome.'

'Neighbours,' Kirsty protested, 'that bothy next door's not fit for neighbours. There's been nobody inside it since we stopped breeding pigs, and the boss sent the pigman packing.'

'It's not the pigman this time,' Finlay assured her. 'It's Italians. Three of them. Prisoners-of-war.'

'*Italians!*' Kirsty gasped. 'Foreigners. Prisoners-of-war.'

Prisoners-of-war, heroic men from far-flung places: the young woman felt a small surge of anticipation rising up within her at the prospect of the widening of her narrow insular world as a farm-worker's wife, almost untouched by the world war that raged around her. She always felt she was missing out on some tremendous event, never more so than when she caught a glimpse of girls of her own age, resplendent in uniform, setting out for places she would never set eyes on. Or when she caught their laughter-filled whispers of a whirling social life, the like of which she had never known.

'Does that mean, does that mean, Finlay, that you'll not be needing us for stooking the sheaves?' She could interpret the anxiety in Kirsty's voice. True enough the women would have preferred minding their homes to the darg in the fields. But, as Finlay was always pointing out, 'Tenpence an hour is not to be sneezed at.'

'Devil the bit of it, Kirsty. From what I hear tell of the Italians, they're none too keen when it comes to bending their backs, and you'd better get the scrubbing brush going,' Finlay advised the young woman, 'and get that bothy cleaned up for the Italians. It will help to make up for the loss of your wages. Kirsty there can give you a hand if she likes,' he suggested, as he turned to go.

'Not *me*,' Kirsty shouted after his disappearing back. 'I've got better things to do than wait hand and foot on a bunch of foreigners.'

3

Slamming her door behind her, Kirsty took her resentment inside the house, and immediately thrust it out again with her bairns. Bundling them threateningly through the door, 'Late for school again,' she warned them, '*another* morning.'

*　　　　　*　　　　　*

Scarfed, hooded, and belted, the bairns stood on the doorstep, momentarily unsure of their bearings, until Alick, spying the snail, shot forward to pounce on it.

> *'Snail Snail*
> *Put out your horn'*

he chanted to the small captive, imprisoned in his hand. Mornings like this the young woman remembered from her own not-so-distant childhood, always lured the snails from the safety of their hiding places, to creep along the highways of danger.

> *'And I will give you*
> *A barley corn'*

she sang across to the bairns, concluding their chant for them. Too grown-up now, though, to intrude on the small miracle that she knew was happening before their eyes, the tremulous appearance of the

4

snail's tiny horns, at the first touch of a human hand.

'Are you lot *still* there?' Kirsty demanded from her doorstep, dissolving the spell, and sending the bairns plunging up through the bracken.

✳   ✳   ✳

'God knows what *she'll* think of the Italians.' Taking her attention off the bairns, Kirsty directed it now to Elspeth, making her way down the hill from her croft at Achullen.

Of all their small community, Elspeth was the only one involved in and affected by the war. Engaged to Callum, a Scots-Canadian, to be married when the war was over, to go to Canada, to live forever. A fine place for Scots to settle in, Elspeth had always maintained. For, as she had often pointed out to the young woman, 'You could work your fingers to the bone, on a small croft like Achullen, and not earn enough to buy the six foot of earth to bury yourself in, when it was all over and done with. But in *Canada* now . . .'

It was after Callum was reported missing at Monte Cassino in Italy that Elspeth had stopped speaking about Canada; and the young woman had never since mentioned Canada to Elspeth. It was as if a whole continent had suddenly disappeared out of their ken.

She missed the 'speaks' though. The fine long

5

'speaks' herself and Elspeth had shared, when Canada existed. Not that the young woman herself had been able to add much to Elspeth's knowledge of it. Remembering only how one of the boys in the orphanage where she had been brought up went to Canada to work on a farm. . . . 'He had a new tin trunk, Elspeth, we all envied him. Going way on a ship, I mean. He was so excited. We envied that too. Then, on the morning he left, he started to cry. I couldn't understand the reason for such tears. Not until the day I left the orphanage myself. Not even then. For I cried too, and I didn't know what I was crying for. . . .'

Elspeth's excitement had also affected the young woman. 'O, Elspeth. You *are* lucky. . . .' Her envy had been heartfelt.

'You'll come and see me,' Elspeth had suggested. Half-teasing, half-serious. 'When your boat comes in. . . .'

But she herself knew that she would never see Canada. 'Nor anywhere else, Elspeth. Just Scotland. . . .'

'*Nonsense,*' Elspeth had reproved her. 'Stuff and nonsense. You're but young yet, lassie. You've got the whole world in front of you yet. . . .'

She had thought that too. Before she was married. She had thought she could go anywhere. Go everywhere, do anything. Do everything . . . 'Not now though Elspeth,' she had confided. 'It's all different now. Being married, I mean . . .'

6

✳   ✳   ✳

'You've *got* to laugh,' Kirsty said, as they watched Elspeth, her old waterproof coat flapping wide in the wind, striding down the hill towards them. The staff she always carried for the steep climb back lashing out at the bracken, clearing the way for the imperious passage of a queen. Boadicea, from remembered history lessons, taking on flesh at last.

'You've got to laugh,' Kirsty insisted. 'Rain or shine. The same old waterproof. And rain or shine. She never bothers to button it up. You've got to laugh. . . .'

Kirsty, almost devoid of laughter herself, was always urging it on to the young woman. Leaving her puzzled, in serious search of laughter's source. There was nothing funny in the aura of dignity that Elspeth always carried within herself. An independence lacking in the young woman and her neighbouring cottar wives. But then there was a fundamental difference between them. Elspeth worked her *own* small acres of land, although whiles having to eke out her livelihood by helping with the seasonal jobs on the farmer's large acres of land.

Elspeth, as she often claimed, could 'pick and choose', could remain unmoved by Finlay's moods and demands, and be unafraid of telling him 'exactly where *he* gets off'. The young woman envied Elspeth's liberty of choice, her freedom of utterance.

7

＊　　　　　　＊　　　　　　＊

'You're redding up,' Elspeth stared round the bare, dust-filled bothy. 'The pigman's bothy, you're redding it up.'

'For prisoners-of-war,' the young woman said.

'For *Italians*,' Kirsty contradicted. 'Foreigners. Did you ever hear the *like*?' she demanded.

'Italians,' Elspeth echoed, turning to the young woman. 'And *you* are redding up the bothy for *them*. For Italians.'

'*I* refused,' Kirsty claimed. 'When Finlay asked *me*, I just refused. Point blank.'

'Just odd jobs, Elspeth.' Aware now of some inexplicable need to apologise, the young woman heard herself plunging deeper into explanation, felt herself falling deeper into disfavour. 'Little jobs just, getting the grocer's van, a bit of washing sometimes, things like that.'

'Ah well.' Taking a last look round the bothy, Elspeth turned on her heel to go. '*That'll* be worth a bob or two in your pocket.'

'It's only because I live next door,' the young woman pleaded to Elspeth's retreating back. 'That's all, Elspeth, only because I live next door.'

＊　　　　　　＊　　　　　　＊

'Elspeth gave you short shrift,' Kirsty remarked, as they watched her making her way back up the hill.

8

'Not that you can blame her,' she reflected, 'with her Callum missing in Italy. Enough to put you off Italians for life. And *another* thing . . .'

Stifling an impulse to rush up the hill after Elspeth, the young woman let Kirsty's tirade flow over and round her. She hadn't found it easy to comfort Elspeth on the day that Callum was reported missing. Her attempts at consolation had sounded too facile to be true. Even to her own ears. 'But Callum's not dead yet, Elspeth. He's not dead. . . .' Words out of context. Running away with her. 'Callum could still be found. He could still turn up. That sometimes happens. I read about that once. In a book . . .'

How much more difficult it would be to find words for an offence that had neither been committed, nor specifically defined.

She would miss Elspeth's friendship. Elspeth who had tried to initiate her into the strange ways of this new life. Who had taught her to bake. Conjuring up a living entity out of a raw ingredient. 'Lightly now—*lightly*. That scones will never rise. Thumping away at the dough like that. Leave it now. Let it alone. For the love of goodness. Give the dough a chance to *breathe*. . . .'

        *   *   *

'What,' Kirsty began to wonder, as the young woman's husband dipped down into view from the high ridge and led the horse and cart into the turnip field, 'what will *he* have to say about the Italians?' Kirsty knew what *her* man would say about that, she claimed. Only she hadn't given him a chance.

The day that had started out this morning on its everyday course was beginning to take on some new and threatening dimension in the young woman's mind. Leaving her without concrete reply to Kirsty's half-articulated reflections.

Her man, she knew, wouldn't have very much to say about the Italians. Not in words. Always on his own, as a cattleman, and working apart from his fellow farm-workers, he had got out of the way of using words. Sometimes, sometimes she felt he had grown out of the need of words at all. She was learning though to interpret by look and mood. The way her man, himself, could interpret each need and nuance of the dumb beasts he worked amongst.

✳   ✳   ✳

Watching him from a distance, as he topped and tailed the turnips, bending down and straightening up, he seemed to the young woman like a man performing some simple exercise to an easeful rhythm of his own composing. Unlike winter, she remembered, when an agonised tussle, an eternal tug-of-war, waged between himself and a reluctant crop held fast to earth. But the frost had not yet

10

fixed its grip on the days, nor on the crop. Nor on the image of his deftly moving hands.

'I'll get you a turnip for the pot,' she said at last, in reply to Kirsty. 'I'll get it when Alick comes down with his load. Before the frost gets at them.'

✳   ✳   ✳

'Prisoners-of-war. Italians.' Her man stood on the doorstep of the bothy, digesting her information. 'But I thought they were going to bide in the camp over, and just coming here to work—day-to-day.'

'Not this three. They're going to bide in the bothy.'

'And *you're* going to look after them, like?'

'No.' She shook her head, uncertain herself of the demands of her role as 'next door neighbour'. 'I'm just redding up the bothy for them.'

'But why you? What about Kirsty and Meg? Have *they* refused?'

'Kirsty and Meg have got bairns,' she pointed out. The look, tightening up her man's face, setting her off on the wheedle, hating herself for the use of it, and momentarily hating the man, who was the instrument of its use. 'According to Finlay, it's something or nothing. Scrubbing out the bothy, once in a while. Getting the odd bit message off the grocer's van. Just things like that. It'll mean a bit extra for us,' she persuaded, 'to save in the tea caddy. A bit to put by. *That'll* please you.' She could hear

11

the resentment beginning to sound in her voice. 'You're always on about "something to put by".'

✳   ✳   ✳

'Your man didn't seem sore pleased with your news,' Kirsty shouted across from her doorstep. 'No more would mine. If it was *me*.'

'*My* man,' she retaliated, her resentment blowing up into positive anger, '*my* man wouldn't mind if I got down on my knees and cleaned up horses' dung. Not if it would give him "something to put by".'

And that was true, she assured herself, slamming the bothy door behind her, in confirmation of a fact.

Certain facts though, she realised, even before she reached her own door, certain facts were out of context. And not for utterance. Shamed by the realisation, and aware of Kirsty's shocked silence, she turned back with her offering. 'Here's a neep for your broth, Kirsty. The frost hasn't got at it yet.'

Kirsty's wordless acceptance reaffirmed an opinion gathered from experience. Peace offerings by themselves were never enough. Explanation was always an essential accompaniment. 'My man isn't really like that, Kirsty, it's me. It's just me.'

✳   ✳   ✳

Me.

Her image, reflected in the looking-glass above

the sink, gazed back at her. Assessing each other, before breaking into a wide smile of recognition. Absolved by confession, sudden lightness of heart overtook her.

> *'One morning I rose*
> *And looked in the glass'*

she sang to the smiling reflection, that mouthed along with her.

> *'Said I to myself*
> *I'm a handsome young lass*
> *I've plenty of money*
> *To dress me so braw . . .'*

'They're here,' Meg shouted, as herself and Kirsty flashed past the window. 'Your new neighbours. The Italians.'

✷　　　✷　　　✷

They stood, the prisoners, as she had seen the bairns stand this very morning, as if struck to stone by the sudden strangeness of their situation.

'This is Mistress Ainslie,' Finlay elbowed her towards them. 'Your neighbour, next door.' Rapping on her door in an attempt at interpretation. 'She'll keep an eye. Rat-tat-tat. Grocer. Food. Eat. Knock wall. Rat-tat-tat.'

It was hard to tell whether the Italians understood Finlay's frantic miming, or whether they were simply reluctant to bring such a fascinating performance to a close.

Kirsty did that for them. 'Good God, Finlay,' she shouted from the gale end of the Row. 'Good God, man, but you should have been on the stage.'

The laughter of the watching farm-hands swirled up and round, leaving the young woman standing beside the Italians within the circumference of their own unease, for what the Italians had understood was that she had been thrust upon them. And was in some way involved. Neither acceptance nor rejection revealed itself in the blank eyes of their appraisal. Leaving her with the urgent need to appraise herself. And, in the doing, she became suddenly conscious of her mud-splattered wellingtons, of the bag apron that gave no hint of the small waist hidden within it. Sharply aware that she stood neuter and sexless. Clad in the garments of renunciation.

✻   ✻   ✻

The young woman stood envying Kirsty's busyness, the cluck of her hens and the clatter of her pails. The normality of it. She would be glad when the weather settled down into its own season again. When each day had its yoking beginning. And its lowsing ending.

'You'd be better uprooting that muckle clump of rhubarb,' advised Meg, leaning over the gate of Kirsty's yard. 'Spreading all over the place like that. Once it gets inside the ree, it will poison all your hens.'

The moment for advice of any kind was inopportune. And Kirsty rejected it. She would, she declared, as soon dig up her grandmother as uproot the clump of rhubarb.

There was no real acrimony in the exchange between her two neighbours. It was part of a pattern they wove together to relieve the tensions of their long years of proximity.

She, the young woman realised, had become part of the pattern too, leaving her neighbours puzzled by, and pondering upon, a shape and colour that had appeared, as if by accident, amongst them, and was not of their design.

The texture of her own life now seemed to hang suspended by the uncertainty of her new, undefined responsibilities. Shy of intruding on the Italians next door, anxious lest she should miss out on a knock on her wall, yet apprehensive of responding to it, since that first time it happened.

✳   ✳   ✳

'*Buona sera, signora,*' Luigi, alone in the bothy, had greeted her. '*Buona sera.*'

'Hello.' She smiled, recognising the sound of

salutation. '*Parla italiano?*' She shook her head. '*No parla italiano.*'

'French,' she heard herself claiming, starting to dredge words up out of schoolday memory. '*Je parle la langue française.*'

'*Français.* Similar *italiano.*' Luigi flung his arm round her shoulder. 'Similar! Posseeble speak.' But not possible to communicate, she realised, her thoughts lingering on half-forgotten irregular verbs . . . *Je suis. Vous êtes. Nous sommes.*

The transformation the Italians had worked on the bothy took her mind off the frustrations of communication.

'*Madonna!*' Luigi said, following her gaze, fixed on the blue poster above his iron bed. Bowing, crossing himself as he moved forward to lay personal claim on the Mother and Child that gazed down on them both. '*Madonna Mia . . .*'

His apartness, excluding her from some mystery, allowed her time to resort to fantasy. . . . 'That's the *Madonna,*' she would point out to Kirsty and Meg, when she invited them in for a quick looksee at the bothy, which had once belonged to the pigman. 'The Madonna,' she would emphasise, knowing that Kirsty would just think it was the Virgin Mary. She too would bow and cross herself, her explanation of such a performance would be as casual as tongue could sound it. 'That's what Catholics do, Kirsty. That's what she's there for. . . .'

'*Mama Mia.* You like?'

None of the quick words of appreciation—true or false—but always necessary in such circumstances, came to her aid. 'You like? *Mama Mia*?'

'Yes.' She nodded. 'Yes.'

'*Yes.*' Luigi lunged at the word. 'Yes! *Si! Si!* Yes!'

'*Si.*' She had uttered her first word of Italian. 'Posseeble?' His grip tightened on her shoulder, as if all obstacles to communication had been swept away. 'Posseeble you like the jiggy-jig?'

She had never before heard the word jiggy-jig. But instantly understood it. But it was the lack of outrage, of affront, which she had felt such a stark suggestion should have aroused within her, that surprised herself.

'No posseeble me like.' A tone of apology sounding in her voice, as if she had simply rejected an invitation to supper.

'*PERCHE* no posseeble? *Perche* no posseeble you, the jiggy-jig?'

'Husband me.' She explained. Twirling the wedding ring around her finger to prove it. 'Married me.'

She was relieved when the door of the bothy swung open. Grateful for the arrival of Paolo and Umberto. Yet suddenly guilty in their presence. A guilt they themselves seemed to fling over her, as they flung their raincapes over the chairs. Their wordlessness sounding their suspicions.

'You've got an odd lot in there,' Meg greeted

17

her, when she closed the bothy door behind her. 'Not one word of Scots between them.'

'Nor English,' she agreed, turning to stare across the firth. The wind was beginning to blow itself out. The fields on the other side of the water were thrusting themselves into view again. Tomorrow, maybe, they might make a start to the stooking.

'And not before time,' Meg grumbled. *Nothing*, she claimed, got herself so down in the mouth as rain. 'Dinging on and on like this.'

She was right, was Meg. Weather, the young woman was beginning to learn, was never an event. It was always an emotion.

✳   ✳   ✳

'What *are* they seeking now?' her man demanded. For the knocks from the bothy were becoming more frequent, and had begun to irritate him.

'Maybe it's their tilley lamp again. They haven't got the knack of it yet.'

'It's high time they did, then,' her man said. For he'd never seen anybody so slow to pick up the knack of things as the Italians.

They had other 'knacks' though, the young woman had discovered. Paolo, carving wood that was dead into shapes that became alive under the flick of his knife and the curve of his fine brown fingers. Umberto, teaching children in a small village school. The tremendous respect the farm-workers had for teachers was never reflected on Umberto. Luigi. O, Luigi. A barrow-boy from the streets of Naples. She knew instinctively from memories of her own early street-spent, barefoot childhood, how it was for Luigi. Cocking a snook at the whole wide world.

Sometimes, sometimes she wished that a magic carpet would whisk all the farm-workers away to Italy, and set *them* down in an alien place. They wouldn't have the 'knack' of it either!

Even Finlay, her man was saying, was beginning to lose patience with them. The little patience he *did* have. For he never had very much of it. He'd set them in the morning to patch up the old sacks for oats. And had come back after dinner to find they'd glued all the sacks together! The language that was on Finlay when he found out was some-thing terrible, just! The memory of Finlay when 'the language was on him' filled the young woman with laughter.

> *'It was yalla and purple*
> *And violet and blue'*

she sang, grabbing her man to dance him round the kitchen.

> *'Neath the boughs of a rowan tree shady'*

'You'd better see what they're seeking next door,'

19

he warned her, disengaging himself, 'or they'll be knocking on that wall all night. One of these days,' he prophesied, 'they'll pump that tilley lamp up so hard they'll blow themselves and all the rest of the world up with it. Though they shouldn't be needing the lamp, it's not nearly lighting up time yet.'

✳   ✳   ✳

Neither it was, she agreed, when she got out into the night. For they had not yet finished stooking the sheaves. But then the harvest was late this year. The wild ducks were already beginning to take their leave of the land. Soon, the wild geese would go honking through the night. *That*, she remembered, was a sound for a real dark night. Dropping invisible down upon you. Turning in at the bothy, a rabbit started up at her feet, as silently as if one of the little shadows on the road had suddenly picked itself up, and flitted away.

✳   ✳   ✳

Luigi and Paolo were crouched on opposite sides of the fireplace when she reached the bothy.

'Come!' Luigi commanded. 'You *hear*? TIC-A-TIC-A-TIC-A. *Che cosa? Che cosa? TIC-A-TIC!*'

'It's only your clock, Luigi,' she laughed, pointing to the alarm clock on the mantelpiece, 'only your clock.'

'No *clock*!' Grabbing the clock to himself, Luigi scurried to the other end of the bothy. 'No clock!' he insisted. 'You hear now?'

'A beetle, Luigi,' she assured him, straightening up from the wall. 'Just a beetle. Lives inside wood in wall. A death watch beetle,' she added, as if some extension of her words would help comprehension. '*Morte*,' she remembered a word that might be universal.

'*Morte! Che? Che morte? Che . . . ?*' The alarm in Luigi's face confirmed her feeling that death, like jiggy-jig, could be understood in any tongue.

'Nobody *morte*, Luigi, nobody. Just name we speak.'

It was nothing, she told her man. 'I could have got a rabbit for the pot,' she remembered, smiling. 'If only I could have catched it.'

✹   ✹   ✹

The stubble fields crackled like spun glass beneath their feet as they made their way to the gate. The field stood stooked. Golden tents in a serried array.

'That's that, then,' Kirsty said, 'for another year.'

The contentment in her voice reached out to touch the others. As if she had handed each of them a gift of unlimited leisure.

There was nothing, the young woman realised, as they leant over the gate, reviewing the scene of

21

their ended labour, nothing in all the world that could ease your own tiredness like watching others still at work.

'You would think Finlay hadn't another minute to live! The way he's hounding the Italians.' Kirsty didn't blame him for *that*. For they had no idea, she claimed. None at all. 'Look see,' she commanded, 'they're missing the stack every time. The sheaves are slipping off their forks before they reach the stack.'

'Ah, well then.' There was a hint of satisfaction in Meg's voice as they turned to go. '*That'll* give Finlay a few gray hairs. That'll teach him who his real workers are.'

Turning now on the young woman who was lagging behind, Kirsty demanded to know what ailed her, that she had so little say for herself the night. If it was the stooking that had knackered her, then God help her at the lifting of the tatties, Kirsty prophesied. She'd know *then* what tiredness was, walking around for days with a broken back.

It was the thistles, the young woman said, they had started to scratch her all over. There was, Meg agreed, more thistles than corn this year. But it was no wonder the young woman was scratched all over. *Anybody* would be scratched, Kirsty pointed out, if they were daft enough to go to the stooking in a short-sleeved blouse. And a skirt up to their knees. Kirsty had never, she claimed, 'seen the like'. But, by God, the young woman would know all about it when she got into bed the night. The heat of the blankets would see to *that*.

They were right, Kirsty and Meg, and that was the trouble, they were right about everything. And the righter they were the more resentful the young woman became. Their cottar houses, 'tied cottages', only partially described their way of life. They were 'tied' to each other. Dependent on each other, in the very isolation of their habitation.

The change that had come over the young woman since the arrival of the Italians might have escaped their microscopic eyes, if it had been gradual. But it hadn't been gradual. It had overwhelmed her, taking herself by surprise. A key which had opened a door that had never been unlocked. And herself becoming the prisoner, stumbling blind, into the light of a new awareness, bursting out of her body in response to Luigi's admiration, shouted in the fields, whispered in the bothy. . . . *Bella. Bella. Bella ragazza.* . . .

It wasn't for Luigi that she had donned her short-sleeved blouse, or kilted her skirt up to her knees. And Paolo hadn't noticed. She could have been Kirsty or Meg, concealed within their woollen grays.

She ran, now, where once she would have walked, leaving them behind to their own middle-aged pace, ignoring their tight-lipped comments. 'For she could,' they observed, 'fairly shift when the Italians were around. Flaunting her bare legs in front of them. Showing off, just.'

23

They were right about that too, about 'showing off'. It was just that she had never before been aware of all the things she had to 'show off'. . . .

※　　　　　　　※　　　　　　　※

'God almighty, Beel,' Kirsty protested as the tractor roared round the corner sending them scurrying against the dyke. 'You damned nearly had the lot of us head first into the ditch!'

'You wouldn't have drowned,' Beel assured her. 'We drained the ditch the other day.'

'If *Finlay* caught you taking round the corner at a lick like that, burning up the tyres . . .' The threat implied in Kirsty's voice took the grin off Beel's face, reminding him of more serious matters.

'Finlay,' he remembered, shouting down from the tractor, 'Finlay says if you see Elspeth at the grocer's van, you might tell her he's expecting her to lowse to the threshing mill, first thing Tuesday morning.'

'Finlay's got a hope,' Kirsty snapped. 'Some nerve.' Elspeth, she reminded him, had refused to set foot in a field with the Italians, and she for one didn't blame Elspeth for *that*. She would have felt the same herself if her Alick had been missing in Italy.

'Better dead than missing,' Meg concluded. 'You know where you are when you're dead.'

＊　　　　　＊　　　　　＊

'The seaplanes! The seaplanes!'

The bairns, shouting in the distance, quickened their pace. Either they were late, or the bairns had got out of school early.

'The seaplanes! The seaplanes!'

'That damned thing's on the go again.' Meg brushed all interest in the weapons of a world war aside, turning to admonish the excited children. 'Never mind the seaplanes. Get yourselves in amongst the stubble there. And gather up some corn for the hens.'

They were flying low, the seaplanes, skimming huge and heavy across the firth. So heavy, the young woman stood wondering how they could ever raise themselves up into the sky.

'You're just as bad as the bairns,' Kirsty admonished her, 'standing there gooking. As if *your* man wasn't expecting his supper the night.'

＊　　　　　＊　　　　　＊

Out now from the hard brightness, into the dead dimness of her kitchen, the contrast caught at the young woman's throat. And stuck there, tangible. A lump, preventing words from coming out. If words could be found, for the worst thing about working in the fields was getting geared up again, to tackle the work lying undone in the house.

25

> *'Moonlight becomes you*
> *It goes with your hair'*

the singer assured her when she turned on the wireless,

> *'You certainly know*
> *The right thing to wear.'*

She did too, but only in her imagination, and in an absorbed study of Kirsty's mail-order catalogue. But two shillings a week—the limit of the instalments she could afford—defied imagination, and whittled choice down to bare essentials, working boots for her man, wellingtons for herself.

> *'If I say I love you*
> *I want you to know*
> *It isn't because it's moonlight*
> *Though . . .*
> *Moonlight becomes you . . .'*

'You're early, surely.' The unexpected arrival of her man set her off on the attack. 'I'm just this minute in. And the supper's not on yet.'

'A cup of tea will suit me fine.'

His mild acceptance increased her resentment. It was not a fitting apology for an intrusion into her rare moments of privacy. Intrusions that seemed to surround, and close in on her—Kirsty, Meg,

Beel, Finlay, the lee-long day. Himself, the long night.

'The heifer's at the drop of calving,' he said, easing himself down on the settle. 'Her udder's swollen. Gey and big, we could be in for a night of it. It being her first calf, you might take a turn up to the byre later on. I'll maybe need a hand.'

'Aye. All right,' she agreed, wondering where her resentment had disappeared to, and why it had ever been there in the first place.

'You'd be better of the lantern,' he suggested, as he rose to go back to the byre. 'I'll away and fill it up for you.'

      ✽   ✽   ✽

She had no need of the lantern. Real darkness never fell down out of the night. It was when it rose up out of the ground that you could lose your bearings, and yourself.

Besides, she liked walking in the dark. There was something nocturnal in her. Atavistic. Something that had never had a chance.

The reflection of Meg's fire flickered against the window. Enough edge to the nights now for a fire. The time of fires, she remembered, stopping to watch the flames rising up from the burning of the whins, that snapped and crackled in protest to the night.

Unprepared for the voice whispering behind her.

27

'*Cara . . . cara mia . . .*' She turned to confront Luigi. Grasping her by the shoulders, he pulled her against himself. 'Posseeble . . . posseeble . . . one time posseeble . . .' Taken by surprise, anger lent harshness to her voice. '*No* possible. *No* time possible . . .'

'*Scusi, signora. Scusi, scusi, mi scusi.*'

The supplication in Luigi's voice, his instant humble acceptance of rejection dissolved her anger. Fear had done that to Luigi. She knew that, as she watched him clinging to the fence, fumbling his way back to the bothy. Fear always had the power to humiliate.

'I thought I smelt burning.' Flinging open her door, Meg crouched within it, her head thrust forward, peering accusingly out into the night. 'I could swear I smelt burning.'

'Wrong spy, Meg.' The young woman's laughter relieved her tension. 'You're right about *one* thing, though,' she conceded. 'Your nose would be worth five pounds in a pointer pup! They've made a start to burning the whins up at Achullen.'

She arrived at the byre in the nick of time. One of the older calves, overcome by curiosity, had got out of its loose box, hell-bent on making the acquaintance of its newly-born kinsman, to the fury of the cow, butting and lashing out at friend, foe, and all inanimate things alike.

'Hold on to the daft devil,' her man commanded, 'till I get the cow settled.'

A safe place the byre, lacking the competitiveness of all other areas of farm work. No 'knacks'—implying that there were several methods—needed here. There was only one way to milk a cow. And the young woman had mastered it. Only one way to calve a cow, and her man was familiar with it.

A fine place to be born in, the byre. Sweetened by the cows' breaths, and the tang of newly-sliced turnips. The relationship between her man and the brute beasts he worked amongst becoming intimate, at times like these. A warm 'mash' for the cow, a gift for her motherhood with a touch of black treacle added as a treat 'for a good lass'.

The newly-born calf was beginning to find its balance. Staggering to grope under the cow in search of its udder. Licking her calf from end to end, almost knocking it over in an excess of maternal devotion. A pity, the young woman thought, watching her man guiding the calf to its urgent objective, a pity. It was to be a sucker calf, a pity it was a bull calf. Not well enough bred to enjoy a lifetime of lascivious freedom. 'You're a fine calfie,' she assured it, stroking its damp head. 'A fine calfie.' Pity to end up a stirk, for prime beef. But she didn't mention that to the newly-born calf.

'It's lucky in a way though,' she reflected, as herself and her man made their way home from the byre. 'It will be left with its mother. Sucking for a long time.'

'But God help us the day it stops sucking.'

Her man was right, she remembered. The crying of the cow when its calf was weaned would make of the byre a place of lamentation. For endless days.

✳ ✳ ✳

She had spent the whole of yesterday evening on her knees in her yard, untangling her sweet-peas. Persuading them to climb up the tiers of twine she had woven between the posts, in an attempt to give them individuality, to discover this morning that they had defied her efforts, scrambling through each other, their tendrils in a twist, clutching at each other's hair, as if they couldn't bear to grow up apart.

She would, Kirsty suggested, peering over the fence, have been a lot better with a bit of netting wire. For Kirsty 'hoped to God' that the young woman wasn't expecting to win a prize at the flower show in the village 'with rogue sweet-peas. Running riot all over the place'.

She had no intention, the young woman snapped, offended by such unwanted criticism, no intention in the world, of setting foot within a mile of the flower show. Nor of 'exhibiting' sweet-peas.

She *must* go, Kirsty insisted. They *always* went. It was expected. They all went together. The young woman would *have* to put in an appearance. Maybe, maybe she only imagined a tone of desperation in Kirsty's voice. A plea for reinforcement.

It hadn't been imagination. The young woman realised that the moment she stepped inside the marquee. For, although the village lay little more than a mile away from them, the cottar wives had no real part in its integral life. They could have 'dropped in' from another planet, to find themselves invisible, in a marquee. Huddling closely together, they began to wander round the different 'sections', their voices rising loud in praise of each and every exhibit on show. As if the sound of themselves could merge within that of the folk who surrounded them.

'Miss McCarthel, from Burnside, for her foreign mission,' Kirsty whispered as a woman homed towards them, rattling a collection tin. 'She gives herself to the poor.'

She would never, the young woman reflected, confronted by a large, weatherbeaten woman, brown from her felt hat down to her brogues, be asked to give herself to the rich.

'Come *on!*' Kirsty nudged the young woman. Elbowing her towards the home baking section. 'Come on and see how Elspeth got on this year.'

'If she entered, that is,' Meg qualified. 'If she had the heart. Considering . . .'

Elspeth had the heart, and hadn't lost the 'knack'. Two yellow tickets and a red. A first prize and two second prizes adorned Elspeth's entries. Setting their seal on her proficiency as a baker of scones, oatcakes and pancakes.

Elspeth, herself, seen now in a dimension beyond

31

her croft at Achullen, belonging to the parish, accepted by the village. Her five acres of land entitling her to that privilege.

They made no attempt to join Elspeth, chatting easily with a group of her own kind. 'We'll see her the morn. At the butcher's van,' Meg said as they turned away towards the cut flower section. There was a time and place . . . Meg had the sensitivity to recognise both.

'You see what I mean,' Kirsty reminded the young woman as they stood admiring the sweet-pea display. 'Yon things of yours would never have stood a chance!'

But the young woman's mind lingered on *other* folk's sweet-peas. As she stood, eavesdropping on the tale of a miracle, that would, for her, always retain its mystery.

'Madam Beaver isn't *always* reliable,' a lady was assuring a man with a first prize red ticket in his hand. 'Not always true to colour. But *congratulations!* She came true for *you.*'

✳   ✳   ✳

Kirsty's mail order catalogue had taken on a new dimension from the moment Finlay had offered the young woman 'a week's lowsing at the threshing mill. Providing the weather keeps up. Seeing as Elspeth—a contramashious bitch at the best of times—she decided against.'

She had never before lowsed at the threshing mill. An admission that Finlay had swept aside, assuring her that there was nothing to prevent her from trying. Not at the going rate of tenpence an hour. 'And *that*,' he had reminded her, 'was not to be sneezed at.'

Neither it was, the young woman conceded, as she sat studying the pages of the catalogue, which had now assumed its true function. A purveyor of goods, luring a customer, who now had a prospect of purchasing away and beyond the section marked 'footwear'.

Always she had been aware of her potential as a female, given the essential transformation.

> *And you shall walk in silk attire*
> *A chain of gold you shall not lack . . .*

'But why *you*? You've never lowsed at the threshing mill before.'

Her man's reaction to her good news was only to be expected. But never quite condoned. If there was a crock of gold lying ready to be lifted on the other side of Achullen Burn he would 'have his doubts' about reaching it because the burn was in spate.

'What about Kirsty and Meg?' he demanded. 'They've got experience. . . .'

So much experience, the young woman discovered, that they had both rejected Finlay's tenpence an hour. All hell, Kirsty recollected, was let loose at the threshing mill. You could neither see yourself, nor anybody else, for that of it, with the chaff flying all over the place. Into your eyes. And blinding the young woman. You thought the thistles was bad enough, she reminded you. But wait you. Just wait you, till the yavins got at you. You'd be scratching yourself to the bone.

It was her back that lowsing always went for, Meg remembered. She could hardly straighten herself up, after a day at the threshing mill. The hardest tenpence an hour she had ever earned, and never wanted to earn another the like!

Her neither, Kirsty confirmed. Finlay knew better than to seek her! And as for old Randy Rob, him that owned the threshing mill. Eighty, if he was a day. And only two things on his mind in eighty years. And one of them was the threshing mill . . .

'All hell', as Kirsty had described it, was let loose as the traction engine, reeking with smoke, shuddered its way into the corn yard. The threshing mill, rattling and swaying behind it, seemed in a mood to part company with the engine, dragging it unwillingly along, piloted by 'the devil himself'. The young woman's first glimpse of Randy Rob completed Kirsty's impression of hell, as black as his own engine. His curses rose darkly up with the smoke.

'Watch out for Randy Rob there,' Beel advised her, as he rushed past, shouldering the forks. 'He'll have his hand up your skirt the minute you turn your back.'

'Fine lot of micies nesting in the sheaves,' Alick warned her as he passed, bending beneath a burden of empty sacks. 'They'll run as far up your legs as possible!'

'You'd better keep an eye on Possible,' the casual workers suggested, choking on their own laughter.

Only the Italians, isolated by their idleness from the frenzied busyness of all the other workers, seemed to share her bewilderment at the chaos in front of them.

'*Che? Che cosa . . . ?*'

She could find no answer to Luigi's query. No word of reply to the questions asked by his gesticulating hands.

Advice began to pour thick and fast from all airts of the corn yard.

'Back her up, man! Round with her. Round a bit yet! Too far. Too far. Back a bit. Forward!'

Unnerved at last by the contradictions surrounding him, the 'devil' leapt out of the traction engine.

'Where the hell do you want the bloody thing?'

'I could tell you,' Finlay snapped. 'But I'll keep that bit pleasure till next year, when we get our combine harvester.'

'*Non capisco,*' Luigi confided, sidling towards her. '*Me non capisco . . .*'

'Me neither,' she assured Luigi, 'me neither.'

35

※　　　　※　　　　※

The strap that held the knife for cutting the 'bands' that tied the sheaves together had begun to cut into her wrist. It had to be tight, Finlay explained, when he fastened it on to her wrist. 'Else, slack, it will fly off and cut all our throats. It's as sharp as that.'

It needed to be sharp to cut the strong straw 'bands' fast enough to satisfy the 'devil' who fed them into the gaping maw of the threshing mill. Its haste and appetite inexorable. A malevolent creature. Crying out for corn. Its cry changing to a whine the moment she slackened pace, to straighten her back.

'Come on. Come on. Move yourself, quine. Move yourself,' the 'devil' bawled in her ear. 'Keep her going. Keep her going.'

'Fling a stone in her, quine!' Beel shouted from the top of the corn stalk. 'That will slow the bugger down. That will give us a breather.'

Leaping up and out from his mill hole, the 'devil' spurted across to the edge of the mill. 'Try that!' he snarled to Beel. 'Just you try that, my mannie, and you'll blow the whole caboodle up. Yourself along with it!'

※　　　　※　　　　※

The forkers, beginning to tire now, were flinging the sheaves across to her at random, their sharp-

36

ness catching at and cutting her face. Half-blinded with the yavins attacking her from all directions, her rising anger became the only proof of her humanity. Alive only in the mechanical way the threshing mill itself was alive.

'Keep it clear! Keep it clear!' she could hear Finlay urging on the Italians, stumbling blindly around, struggling to clear the windblown chaff.

'Keep it clear, lads. Keep it clear!'

The pity she was beginning to feel for herself extended to, and encompassed, the Italians, setting her apart with them, from all the other workers, who seemed to be so lucky. Moving and living and having their being in a way of life that was familiar to them.

✳   ✳   ✳

'You didn't come home for your dinner, then?' her man greeted her, when she got in from the threshing mill.

'I couldn't, I couldn't move to go anywhere. I just sat at the bottom of a corn stack, hoping to God I'd manage to rise up when the mill started again.'

That, her man pointed out, was just because it was her first time at the threshing mill. She would, he prophesied, find it easier the morn.

Times like these, she couldn't trust her own voice. Obscenities, known and unknown, would have risen up from their deep dark places to blacken out the world. Times like these, fantasy would come to her aid.

> *Fish of the sea*
> *Come listen to me*
> *For I would beg a boon of thee*

Gold?

Aye. All the gold in the world.

Quiet, she would be, when she scattered all the gold in the world at her man's feet.

Here it is. Gold. All the gold in the world. You never need be anxious about money again. . . .

'You'd be the better of a cup of tea,' he suggested. 'I'll put the kettle on. There's no need,' he turned at the scullery door, hesitant, as if in search of words that could penetrate the armour of her silence, 'there's no need to go back to the threshing mill the morn, if you're not feeling up to it. We'll manage. We'll manage fine.'

'It wasn't too bad,' she heard herself assuring him. Disarmed. Pleased and surprised by his rejection of all the gold in the world. 'Finlay was pleased with me. He said I'd the makings of a good lowser. Nearly as good as Elspeth,' she added, as an afterthought. That wasn't quite true, but she would have liked it to have been true.

✳   ✳   ✳

Released at last from the pains and perils of the threshing mill, the young woman squeezed herself onto the wooden form, in a state of expectant euphoria.

'Ladies and gentlemen! Order please!'

Beel, in his new role as master of ceremonies, stood stiff in his Sunday suit with its white starched 'dickey', attempting to bring to heel the workers wandering around, criticising or condoning—according to their frame of mind—the transformation that had changed the familiar barn into the venue for the annual harvest home.

'If *that's* the band,' Kirsty said, drawing their attention to the fiddler and accordionist hovering together by the barn door, 'it's some *band*! You would have thought they could have risen to a piano.'

The entrance of the farmer with his own personal guests lagging behind him brought an order to the barn that Beel, unaided, hadn't managed to achieve.

'Take your partners!' he commanded, with the confidence of one who now had authority behind him. 'Take your partners for the Grand March and Circassian Circle.'

'We'll never hear the end of *that*!' Kirsty hissed as the farmer, stepping forward, offered his arm to Finlay's wife to lead off in the Grand March. 'She'll be bragging about that for months,' Kirsty concluded.

'It's the custom,' Meg pointed out. 'She's the foreman's wife. He leads her off every year.'

'Custom or no custom,' Kirsty insisted, 'she's never got over it. She'll be on and on about it till next year.'

> *'March! March!*
> *Ettrick and Teviotdale*
> *Why my lads dinna ye*
> *March forward in order*
> *March! March!*
> *Eskdale and Liddesdale . . .'*

The martial music, and the marchers, stumping around the barn stirred the young woman into action. 'Come on, Kirsty,' she pleaded. 'You and me. Come on. Let's get ourselves in amongst them.'

The young woman, Kirsty declared, declining the proposed partnership, could make a fool of herself if she liked. That was up to *her*. But she, Kirsty, had no intention of doing likewise, not with 'everybody looking'.

Nobody was 'looking'. They should have gone through life invisible, Kirsty and Meg, their fear of attracting attention to themselves was so deeply rooted.

Even on social occasions like this, neither frill nor ribbon put forth a frivolous claim, no innocent coquetries, no small vanities. It was as if the whole chapter of their youth had been torn from their

40

book, and they had turned the page from child-hood to middle age.

Even so, the young woman was beginning to feel that maybe she *was* over-conspicuous in what had been her choice from Kirsty's catalogue, described as 'a frock in which to go forward into autumn. In a shade that blends with this most colourful season'.

✻   ✻   ✻

The marchers, having finished applauding them-selves, now scrambled around trying to reclaim their former places on the forms. For it was by no means certain that having given up your place you could claim it again. Which was why, Meg pointed out, as they listened to territorial disputes rising up around them, *they* had been wise to have simply sat on their backsides, and held on to their places.

'To give you all a chance to get your wind back,' Beel announced, 'I will now call for a song. On our good neighbour, Mistress Fraser. A song, Kirsty. If *you* please!'

' "The Barley Riggs", Kirsty,' the workers urged. 'Come on, Kirsty. Give us "The Barley Riggs" '—starting up the chorus themselves, to encourage the song of their choice.

'One singer, one song,' Beel reminded them sharply, turning towards Kirsty. 'Right then, Kirsty. Is't to be "The Barley Riggs"?'

' "The Rowan Tree"!' Rising to her feet, Meg

made Kirsty's mind up for her, momentarily depriving Beel of ceremonial authority. 'Kirsty, Mistress Fraser, will render "The Rowan Tree"!'

> *'Thy leaves were aye the first o' spring*
> *Thy flooers the summer's pride*
> *There wasna sic a bonnie tree*
> *In a' the countryside . . .'*

Strange, now that everybody *was* looking, Kirsty seemed unaware. Maybe you could face the whole world, and its stares, when you could do something to perfection. The young woman hadn't known that Kirsty could sing. Not as she was singing now. Her voice, clear and sweet, rising up through the stillness that had come over the barn. If Kirsty and me could just sing to each other, she thought. Instead of speaking. We'd never contradict each other again.

> *'So fair wert thou in summer time*
> *Wi' a' thy clusters white*
> *How rich wert thou . . .'*

There had been a rowan tree at the gale of her grandmother's house. And a bourtree at the back of it. As a city child, come to visit, she couldn't tell the difference between the two trees, in summer, their white flowering time. But to Grandmother, the rowan tree had been 'special', guarding the house within it from evil.

42

Strange, that Grandmother, who said prayers every night, and believed in them, had just as much faith in the rowan tree, at the gale end of her house. Maybe not so strange after all. The shadow of paganism. And its substance. Grandmother, suspended between Heaven and earth, had been making sure of both worlds. . . .

'How rich wert thou in autumn dress
Wi' berries red and bright . . .'

'She used to sing all by herself in the kirk,' Meg whispered, as Kirsty made her way back to them. 'She did that. My, but Kirsty could sing.'

' "Corn Riggs and Barley Riggs"!' Dave Smollet shouted, crashing through the blank that Kirsty's song had left behind. 'No excuses now. You all know the words.'

'Corn riggs and barley riggs
And corn riggs are bonnie'

Swaying together along the forms, stamping their feet, they sang as if in a sudden burst of release.

'I have been blithe wi' comrades dear
I have been merry drinking
I have been joyful gathering gear
I have been happy thinking

'But of a' the pleasures e'er I kent
Tho' three times doubled fairly
That happy nicht was worth them a'
Amang the riggs wi' Annie

'Corn riggs and barley riggs
Corn riggs are bonnie . . .'

'Now that *that* lot are making themselves scarce,' Meg confided, as the farmer and his guests turned at the barn door, raising their arms in a wordless gesture that could have been one of benediction, or farewell, 'we'll see some fun! The flasks will be whipped from the men's hip pockets. And Beel will be legless before the night's out.'

'On your feet!' Finlay had now stepped swiftly into the role of mine host and master of ceremonies. 'Take your partners for an eightsome reel. You too, Meg! And you, Looeeshee! You can give Meg a birl or two. . . .' For the first time the young woman became aware of Luigi, hovering on the threshold of the barn, as if unsure of his reception. As a fellow-worker, or as a prisoner-of-war.

She would dance now, despite Meg, despite Kirsty. With her man. But she would dance. For the joy of displaying her new frock. For the pride of 'showing off' her 'steps'. For the appreciation of Paolo.

'The cheek of Finlay,' Meg was protesting. 'Thinking *I* would dance with the Italian, and the

44

cheek of the Looeeshee one. Forcing himself *here* in the first place. I'll say that for the other two Italians. They *know* their place.'

Strange, for once, and suddenly, she felt in agreement with Meg. A feeling of dislike for Luigi, standing grinning in the doorway, took hold of her. He wasn't Paolo.

'Come on, quine. On your feet. *We'll* show them.' Mellowed by the contents of the flask in his hip pocket, Finlay advanced towards her, 'We'll show them, quine!'

*   *   *

'And you showed them right enough,' Kirsty accused, as the three of them walked back together to the Cottar Row. 'Your petticoat flying above your head, flinging yourself about the barn like yon.'

'It was Finlay's fault. You saw that for yourselves. He was trying to birl me off my feet.'

'He wouldn't have danced with one of *us*,' Kirsty pointed out, 'if he hadn't had a good dram inside of him.'

*   *   *

She *should* have said it, she reminded herself, as she watched Kirsty and Meg disappear round the gale end. She had meant to say it, wanted to say it . . . O Kirsty, but you sang right bonnie the nicht.

45

Wi' a' thy clusters white
How rich wert thou
In autumn dress

The sound of laughter drifted across from the bothy. Bicycles, slanted against its walls, proved that Paolo and Umberto were celebrating the end of harvest in their own way, with their own kind from the main camp. Stiffening at the sound of approaching footsteps, the young woman, preparing to confront and dismiss Luigi, turned at the sound of her man's voice. . . .

'That was a real good night. Finlay and Beel were in fine form.'

'Aye,' she agreed, making no mention of the fact that Paolo hadn't set eyes on a frock that 'vied with the colours of autumn'.

✳   ✳   ✳

'That's that, then. For another year.' The finality of Kirsty's observation held within it a tone of regret, as they stood together, watching the men clearing out the barn after the harvest home. Sounding to the young woman as if the whole of their year could be concentrated into the essence of a single day.

'There's Christmas,' she ventured, in an effort to salvage something out of the bleak prospect.

But Christmas, as Meg pointed out, wasn't the same. Except for the bairns.

'Hogmanay, then.'

'You can keep your Hogmanay,' Kirsty snapped, rejecting Hogmanay as if the young woman herself had invented that festival. As far as Kirsty was concerned, Hogmanay 'just makes work for the wives. And beasts of the men'.

'Sing horse. And you'll get corn,' Meg advised Finlay as he came into sight. Weaving from one side of the grass verge to the other, examining pot-holes in the road that led to the loft.

'That damned lorries again!' he grumbled, turning into the field. 'They'll have no bloody road left!'

That, as Kirsty explained, was 'the bee in Finlay's bonnet'. For a constant war waged between Finlay and the lorry drivers from the town. No quarter given, no battle either won or lost. The weight of the lorries, and the speed of their drivers, churning up the stones and howking great holes in the road, leaving the task of filling them up again to the men on the farm. A task never to their liking. And one they considered, and rightly in *Kirsty's* opinion, outwith their particular territory. There would, she prophesied, 'be hell to pay now that the lorries would be coming with winter feed for the cattle. And here comes the *first* of them!'

'You stupid-looking bugger!' Finlay shouted, waving his fist under the nose of the driver whose lorry slanted precariously between the ditch and the bend of the road, 'I've gotten a mind to put my foot up

47

your backside and getting *you* down into filling up this road. My men have better things to do than kirn about with holes in the road. They're not bloody navvies. You stupid . . .'

'Bugger! *Stupido* . . .' Darting out from amongst the men, Luigi had come to Finlay's support. 'Bugger! *Stupido!*'

'That's *it*, Looeeshee. Go on. *You* tell them.'

'Bloody wop!' Stung into retaliation by the intervention of Luigi, the driver leapt down from his cab. 'Italian bastard!'

'Put a finger on that man,' Finlay warned the driver. 'Just one finger and you can say fareweel to that damned lorry of your. For it's an *ambulance* you'll be needing, my mannie.'

       ✻   ✻   ✻

There would be no lifting of the tatties today, nor the morn, not if the rain kept dinging on like this. But the real storm, the furious conflict between the wind and the rain, was being waged high over the firth. For the earth itself never put up a fight against the vagary of such weather, but laid itself down, flat and desolate, in submission.

It had upset Kirsty, her bairns 'let off' school to help with the 'lifting' . . . 'In and out amongst her feet'.

'Keep away from that bothy!' Her voice rose in warning to the bairns. 'I've told you before. And will not be telling you again. Keep away from the *Italians*!'

Bird-like, the bairns seemed to the young woman. Hopping cautiously but curiously up to peep through the bothy window. Fluttering away in a startled group as their mother's threats became louder.

'This weather,' Kirsty confided to the young woman, 'will suit the Italians. Nothing to do but sit on their backsides in the bothy. It will fair suit them.'

⁂

It suited the terns, taking up its challenge, scudding high across the firth, wheeling defiantly round in the teeth of the wind, filling them out with white pride, like pictures the young woman had seen of sailing ships in olden times. Hard to tell whether the crying of the terns sounded distress or delight. Delight, she liked to think, as she watched them zooming down and rising high. Like fighter planes, across the firth.

'Nothing for look,' Luigi lamented, when she went into the bothy with their milk, where he stood gazing out of the window to the rain-blurred hill. 'In Scotland, nothing for look. Tatties and turnips. Wind and rain. Wind. The bloody wind.'

They said that pigs could see the wind. Whiles, the young woman had the feeling that Luigi could 'see' the wind, the feud between himself and the wind becoming almost personal. This she could understand. Time and again the wind had sent herself and Kirsty and Meg on a futile search for the towels and pillowslips it had filched from their washing lines. To be found again, an autumn away, hidden and discoloured beneath the bramble bushes. You must never, she remembered, pick the brambles when the Devil spits upon them. . . .

But it was the grapes that Luigi was crying out for now. Mourning their loss . . . 'No-one get grapes for *Mama mia*. No *vino*. No sun. No *divertimento*. Plenty grapes, Napoli. *Molto, molto*. Plenty sun. Plenty *vino*. Plenty, plenty, Napoli.'

She was almost tempted to let her mind linger in his sunlit wine-drenched land, but her voice rose in defence of her own countryside. 'Not *always* wind, Scotland, Luigi. Not always rain. You *wait*!' she urged. 'You *see*! You look on hill when heather comes. September . . .'

She had not yet learned to avoid the pitfalls that could send Luigi pacing the floor in a gloom of anger, had not yet learned to avoid pinpointing time, bringing its passing to his attention.

'*Settembre. Quando? Quando? Quando? Quando finita la guerra? Quando? Quando? Mama Mia!*'

She could sense the wordless reproach of the others. The rustling of the pages of Umberto's book. Paolo's renewed attack on his blocks of wood.

'You make, Paolo. You finish?' Moving towards him, she stretched to touch the wooden figure in his hands. The way she might reach out at passing jetsam, after a shipwreck. 'You make, Paolo. Beautiful. . . .'

'Paolo *stupido*,' Luigi accused, diverting his anger. '*Molto stupido*. Make for *bambini*. Not for sell. Friends camp. Giovanni. Giuseppe. Plenty make. The rings. Brooches. For sell. For money, for play cards. For cigarettes. Paolo? No. No sell. *Stupido*. . . .'

✸   ✸   ✸

The weather had settled itself at last. Dry with a touch of frost. Promising fine for the tattie howking. Another landscape lost, the young woman realised, staring down on a field of withered tattie shaws. Her eyes had become accustomed to the purple blaze and yellow bloom of the tattie field in flower. She would miss that.

'Tatties,' she shouted to Luigi, as he trundled past in the bogie. 'Tatties for ever!' It was one of their jokes, bridging the difference between their staple diets. God alone knew how the Italians could stomach macaroni, Meg always declared. Since she herself 'couldn't stomach the stuff!' An avowal that puzzled the young woman, since Meg frankly boasted of never having tasted it.

Maybe God *did* have something to do with it, she remembered, the memory smiling her. They liked cheese, the Italians, but not calfie's cheese,

51

the cheese she herself made from the first yield of the cow's milk after calving. '*Che cosa? Che?*' Luigi would query, gazing down in bewilderment on her blood-red offering. Crossing himself as he gazed. A ritual that seemed to her not only a recognition of the presence of God, but a protection against potential Evil.

✻   ✻   ✻

Kirsty and Meg, shaking the mats outside their doors, emptying their ash around the shrubs in their yards, were not yet ready to set off for the tattie field. The unreadiness of reluctance to leave their homes and housework behind.

Their bairns were on their way, though. Banging on their pails as they raced past her door. Grabbing up her own pail, the young woman ran to catch up with them.

> *O we can play on the big bass drum*
> *And this is the way we do it!*
> *Bang! Bang! Bang!*
> *On the big bass drum*
> *And this is the music to it!*

She would have little breath for singing, Kirsty informed the young woman when herself and Meg got down to the field, Aye, would she. By the time this day was done. *They* had better things to do,

52

herself and Meg, than caper around with the bairns. *Or* to fash, putting curlers in their hair for tattie howking. She couldn't even *sleep* in the things, Meg declared, she just turned and tossed all night. Still, Kirsty concluded ominously, they knew what all the palaver was in aid of. They weren't born yesterday.

So. They *knew*. They had noticed. Strange that the young woman could still delude herself, that the changes coming over her had not been apparent to others.

'*Bella*,' Luigi greeted her, as she walked towards the tattie pit. '*Bella. Bella.*'

Paolo, squatting on his upturned pail, was oblivious to her presence. All her preparation, her keen anticipation of the early morning, fell away from her. Appreciation, like the rising wind, was coming from the wrong direction.

Reeshling through the tattie shaws to the pit, Kirsty and Meg now arrived at the point of debate. The sight of the Italians sitting at ease sent them straight into the attack.

The riddling of the small tatties for next year's seed had hitherto been Elspeth's job. Now that there was no Elspeth on the 'squad', it was but *right* that it should fall to one of themselves, since it was, after all, 'a *woman's* job'.

'Or a bairn's,' Beel reminded them, backing his tractor away from the pit.

There were times, right enough, when Beel got all above himself. This was threatening to be one of them. They would, Kirsty reminded him, 'see what *Finlay* had to say about that. Him being the boss.'

His authority confirmed, Finlay put it to immediate purpose.

The best thing, he suggested, the squad could do was just to get hold of their pails. And get themselves to the top of the drills. As fast as maybe.

'When the digger's ready,' Kirsty pointed out with some degree of satisfaction. 'By the looks of it, it will never be ready.' An observation which passed unchallenged. For it was true. And it was familiar. No matter, no matter how much time and work was spent in getting the mechanical machinery 'right and ready' for their seasonal tasks, they seemed to rear themselves up in objection the moment they were confronted by their tasks.

They could, the women agreed regretfully, as they eased themselves down amongst the straw, prepared for a long wait, have had their washing out on the line, on a good day like this. Not much drying in it. But the wind was still rising, with that touch of frost in it that always seemed to whiten the sheets.

'That'll be my new catalogue,' Kirsty claimed, when they spied Postie leaning her bicycle up against the dyke. 'You can save Postie's legs for her,' she shouted to the bairns, brandishing the withered shaws as they chased each other round the pit. 'You can get my catalogue.'

'Posseeble *me*!' Luigi had leapt to his feet, stumbling through the tattie shaws. 'Posseeble *lettera* ME. Posseeble . . .'

Never expectant of letters herself, the young woman had taken no notice of the coming of the mail, until the Italians came, finding herself now looking for letters, through *their* eyes.

'*Domani*, Luigi,' she would try to console in the long, letterless days. 'Letter *domani*. Maybe letter *domani*.'

'*Domani. Domani. Sempre domani!*' He was right about that, her habit of holding out a vague promise of tomorrow, for the certain disappointment of today.

'No *lettera*. No *lettera* Mama Mia. One month, two month, *five* month. No *lettera*. Maybe *morte*. *Mama Mia* . . .' Directing his emotion from herself to the Madonna on the wall, a source of more powerful consolation, with a greater capacity to bear the brunt of the blame. . . .

'Nobody get *vino* for *Mama Mia*. No for *mangiare*. Nobody for work for *Mama Mia* . . . *Quando*, *QUANDO finita la guerra?* . . .'

Times like these, Paolo huddled on his stool, Umberto hidden behind a book, it seemed as if Luigi had deprived them of all *their* emotion, had grabbed it to himself, and shook it fist-high in the face of Heaven and of the Madonna.

✻   ✻   ✻

The digger in working order at last, Finlay loped towards them, where they stood determined at the tattie pit. What ailed them all then, what was the trouble now, he demanded. 'The riddling,' Meg said. 'A woman's job. Not right that the Italians should have it.'

'The Italians,' Finlay assured her, 'don't want your bloody jobs. The Italians, poor buggers, couldn't tell the difference between a tattie shaw and a tattie tuber, never mind wanting to riddle the rooshac tatties.' The Italians would do just as they were told, Finlay confirmed, his patience beginning to desert him. And so would the women, he prophesied, if they wanted to keep their jobs, that was. And lucky to have jobs at all, with land girls springing up all over the place, just waiting for the chance to jump into their shoes.

'That'll be right,' Kirsty muttered, as they scrambled to collect their pails. 'No land girl on this earth would work under Finlay.' And if she *did*, Kirsty concluded, she would be as daft as they themselves were.

> *'Bless them all*
> *Bless them all*
> *The long and the short*
> *And the tall'*

'I hope you've lifted that drill clean,' Finlay shouted, as the young woman sang past him, on

56

the way to the top of the field to start on a new rigg.

'Clean as a whistle, Finlay,' she assured him.

'Just you get yourself back here,' Finlay commanded, 'and give Meg and Kirsty a hand to finish *their* drills.'

She had forgotten. In the release of spirit that had overtaken her, she had forgotten the unwritten rule, made by themselves, for themselves, to help each other to keep up the same working pace. A mutual insurance against days when they 'didn't feel up to it', against the threat of old age, and the ailments it brought in its wake. She had forgotten. Old age seemed so far away from herself. And tiredness was still something outwith her ken.

'We'll manage, Finlay,' Meg shouted from her drill. 'We've managed before by ourselves. We'll manage again.'

＊　　　　＊　　　　＊

It always took a little time to work your way back into the fold, to get on friendly terms with Meg and Kirsty again. Sometimes, sometimes the young woman felt that she had to humour the whole wide world. Her man. Kirsty and Meg. The Italians. Delving within herself for words that might atone for her breach of the Rule, she could feel the loss of her own identity.

'*They* didn't break their backs the day,' she said,

as Paolo and Umberto mounted their bicycles, and went freewheeling past them down the road.

'Whiles,' Meg reflected, as they watched the Italians disappear, 'whiles, I feel it's me, myself, that's the prisoner. Hardly ever getting away from the place. The Italians, now, they're always on top of the road. Always going somewhere. If it's not off to Mass, as they call it, it's up and away to confession. But, no doubt, they've got plenty to confess.'

'*You* should become a Catholic then, Meg,' the young woman suggested teasingly. 'Then *you* could be up and off.'

If, Meg said, firmly rejecting the suggestion, *if* she ever had anything to confess, her tone implying that was highly unlikely, she would go straight to her Maker to do so. Not to some Popish priest who was only a man, after all.

✻   ✻   ✻

'It's not dinner time yet,' the young woman warned, as Luigi huddled past her door. 'It's not nine o'clock yet.' Another 'off day' for Luigi.

She was beginning to read the signals that brought them on. Mist as thick as a wall had closed itself around the farm, which took its mood from the weather, just as it took its colour from the passing seasons. The fog had kept the sun from setting, and the moon from rising, holding it, white and startled, suspended in the sky. Only the dull and distant hammering of the men repairing the fences gave witness to a world that was still inhabited. An 'odd job' day. Neither here nor there. With neither positive beginning nor satisfying ending.

'Me sick. *Soffrire* me,' Luigi mumbled over his shoulder. Turning at the bothy door to assure her that he had Finlay's permission to get off work, his state of mind sounding in the defiance of his voice. A defiance that found its echo in the anger beginning to rise up in herself, as she waited for the knock that was sure to come.

'Though I speak with the tongues of men and of angels', she remembered. For she had always liked to hear the minister expounding on that, though all she wanted now was a down-to-earth working knowledge of Italian, so that she could berate Luigi in his own tongue: 'You are cunning. You get off work to get at me alone. You think I am vulnerable, sorry because you didn't get a letter. You are cunning. . . .'

She didn't know the word for sly or cunning, when the knock came. 'No possible' was all that she could find to say. All that Luigi could understand. . . .

'No possible.'

'Me sick. Me *soffrire*. Too much *soffrire* me. *One* time. One time posseeble?'

'No possible, Luigi. No one time possible.'

'*Paolo* posseeble! Posseeble *Paolo*. Paolo you like.'

Left without words in any language at all, she realised that her feeling for Paolo was transparent.

'What about the Italians' milk?' her man was asking. 'Are you not taking it in to them then?'

'In a minute. They can wait. Surely to God they can wait a *minute*!'

Her outburst was not against her man, taken unaware, but a protest against fear. A fear that was almost physical. Like a thin, yellow worm, beginning to crawl around inside her. Her own man, her own kitchen, had taken on a sudden safety that she felt reluctant to leave.

✳   ✳   ✳

Luigi's 'off day' had infected the bothy, as she knew it would.

'Too much *sick* Luigi.' Vehemence, rare in Paolo, took her by surprise, although not directed at herself but intended for Luigi. 'Me sick,' he claimed. 'Umberto sick. Everybody sick. Me work. Umberto work. Sick similar.'

His resentment would never reach Luigi, would never penetrate. Despair had taken on the tangible form of a man lying face downwards on a bed, hidden by blankets.

'*Domani* Luigi work. *Domani* Luigi joke. Plenty joke. *Domani*,' Paolo informed Umberto as they went to the table. 'Today. *No* joke. No work.' Two prisoners sat down together at the table. They had eliminated the third.

A lack of mutual compassion was an aspect that was new to the young woman struggling to find words to overcome it. She knew them all right. Surely. *Surely* since you are all in the same boat. Surely . . .

But she hadn't forgotten the Italian for that.

'*Domani*. Luigi OK today. No like. *Me* no like. *Umberto* no like. *Soffrire* similar . . .'

Shoving his plate away from him, and clattering his knife and fork on the table, Paolo leapt to his feet, and retreated to his stool by the fire, cupping his down-bent head in his hands. 'Me too. Me *soffrire*.'

'Eat, Paolo.' She tried to persuade him. '*Mange*. Eat, Paolo.'

Maybe, maybe compassion had another side to itself. Not just an understanding of suffering, but an involvement with it.

Luigi had gone beyond captivity. Umberto, eating calmly at the table, held himself aloof from it. There were only two prisoners in the bothy now.

But she wasn't a prisoner, not a *real* one. All *she* had to do was just turn around and walk out. It was her legs that refused to take her to freedom. She needed the password for that. She hadn't got it, but knew it was necessary. The knock on the bothy wall ended her search. 'Husband,' she said. 'Married me. Knocking for me.'

61

'There should never be three,' she reflected when she got back to the safety of her kitchen. 'Never three.'

'Three what?' her man asked, puzzled.

'Three prisoners. Three of anything.'

Nobody knew that better than herself—the whole cottar world knew that—they always disliked to find themselves in a Cottar Row of three houses. For there was always one left out. . . .

Come to think of it though, where would Meg and Kirsty be in those times when they 'fell out' with each other if they hadn't got herself as the go-between. The recipient of their 'honest opinions' of each other. The ultimate bearer of the olive branch, which both wanted to extend but for which each claimed that she had 'too much pride'. Maybe, maybe three in such confined, close-knit circumstances was essential after all. A buffer was needed. She was beginning to recognise Umberto, the school-teacher's role.

> *Now is the hour*
> *That we collect our pay*

The young woman sang out as herself and Kirsty waited for Meg, kirning about amongst the shrubs at her door. Meg was always like that, Kirsty complained, always pretending that she was in no hurry for her wages. All put on, just. Pretending that she wasn't as hard up as the rest of them.

If she had *one* regret, Meg confided, when they got to her door, it was this jasmine bush. Always in leaf. Never in flower. Her one wish, that she should have remembered to take the jasmine from her last cottar house. She had grown it herself, from a cutting no bigger than her finger. But then, you knew yourselves what 'flitting' was like. By the time she'd got her bit sticks furniture loaded up on the cart, the mare was fit to bolt with all the clang and clatter going on around her. That was her one wish. For she never had jasmine that bloomed like yon. Never before, nor since.

Too small a wish for such a long regret. You needed magic for the granting of a *real* wish. For the gaining of something outwith the bounds of probability. The young woman was almost tempted to reveal the heart and matter of a *real* wish. . . .

One week. Just one. Out of all my life. To spend with Paolo. Then I could live fine for the rest of my life with my own man.

'Canada,' she told them. 'That's *my* one wish. I'd like to see Canada.' And near enough true, it was distance that made a lie of it. Canada was a long way from a village near Rome. Instantly regretting, not the lie, but the utterance of it. For it brought Elspeth immediately to mind. It wasn't likely that Elspeth would set foot in Canada now,

Kirsty remembered. Nor that she would set foot in the farm again, not with the Italians around.

'It wasn't the Italians' fault,' the young woman ventured. 'Not *our* Italians. They weren't even *at* Monte Cassino.'

'*Our* Italians.' Kirsty, considering the claim, sniffed in rejection.

'They're Italians all the same,' Meg snapped, remembering Abyssinia. Minding it, she said, as clear as anything. Because the minister had got so worked up about it in his sermon, 'he nearly flung himself out of the pulpit. With the rage that was on him.'

The young woman, ignorant of what had happened in Abyssinia, let her thoughts touch warily down on the here and now. On that other difficulty that had pushed itself into her days, the meetings with Elspeth when the vans came round. Grocer. Butcher. Baker. Dreaded days of the week. Not that Elspeth ever uttered. It was her silence that hurt.

✳   ✳   ✳

They must have come into a fortune, Finlay deduced, as he handed them their wages. For they had been in no hurry to collect them. Still. If *they* didn't want their money, that was all right by him. He could do fine with it. Himself, apparently, not being endowed with *their* worldly wealth. His one fear *was*, now that they'd got their hand on it, they would make straight for The Tappit Hen, and get drunk.

Finlay would have his little joke, they agreed, as they made their way back to the Cottar Row. For none of them had ever set foot in a pub. They left that to the women of the town. Still, they concluded, Finlay wasn't all that bad. Not when you got to the bottom of him. He hadn't even kept that hour off her, Meg remembered. That time she had to wait in for the doctor for Jamie's shingles. She had worked for a foreman once who kept ten minutes off your pay if you didn't turn up 'on the dot'!

Although they had never tasted drink, itself, the wage packets, tucked deep down inside their coat pockets, always had an intoxicating effect on them. Their *own* money. Earned by *themselves*. Giving them the illusion of independence. To be spent, in illusory moments like these, on themselves. In a conspiracy of spirit.

> *'From the bonnie bells of heather*
> *We brewed ale in auld lang syne'*

The young woman started to sing in an uprush of feeling that had come over them. Each for the other.

> *'It was sweeter far than honey*
> *It was stronger far than wine . . .'*

They hadn't really seen the heather this year, Meg

reminded them, tugging them to a standstill, to reflect on the enormity of such a loss. They'd just never got the length of the hill. Time had flown by so fast. And they had no idea where it had gone. There would be other times though. The hill would always be there. At least they had managed to pick the blackberries. A lesser pleasure, the young woman remembered. Riving and tugging amongst the thorny bushes, to emerge as fretful as porcupines. Linking arms together again, they set off for the Cottar Row.

> *It was sweeter far than honey*
> *It was stronger far than wine.*

The young woman was, on this night, the most affluent wife in the Cottar Row, with silver in the tea caddy. And paper money under the mattress.

Snecking her door, she drew her curtains to shut out the inquisitive eye of the night before she settled down at the kitchen table to help her man with the count. They knew to sixpence how much the tea caddy contained. And to a pound how much lay under the mattress. But this was the night of the grand total, with its addition of harvest money. Mill money. And tattie money. . . . 'All the gold in the world', she remembered. Here it was, spread out in front of them. It had taken on a different dimension from past nights of reckoning though, and become a kind of atonement for the guilt she felt for the betrayal of her feelings towards her man. If he had been a bad man, she thought as she watched him, quiet and serious, smoothing out the crumpled bank notes, or if only he had been her father, or even her brother . . . Jumping up from the table, she could hear herself beginning to gabble. She had worked hard at the threshing mill, hadn't she now? Even Finlay admitted that. She would work there again. It was well worth it. Wasn't it? Kirsty and Meg didn't have as much money as *she* had the night. But then, they hadn't worked as hard as her. Wasn't that right?

'Aye,' her man agreed. That was right, that was right enough. Advising her to 'settle yourself down now. Or you'll put me clean off the count.' The real joy of the count lay in the spending of the total.

'Curtains,' she suggested. 'New curtains. Like the ones Kirsty got out of her catalogue.'

There was nothing wrong with the curtains they had, her man pointed out. They were more in need of new planks to shore up the old hen-house.

'Cockerels, then. Six-week-old cockerels, for fattening up. To sell to the butcher's van at Christmas.'

'Some late for that,' her man reminded her, 'with Christmas only weeks away.'

'What about bikes, then? Two second-hand bikes.'

He saw no need for bikes either. 'Not when the milk lorry runs us into town. On our day off.'

That was only once a month, she protested. There were other times. Other places to see.

Never as far as Napoli, though. Never as far as Roma.

Extra money never bought 'extra' things, she realised, as she let the coins trickle through her fingers, having lost interest in their purchasing power. It came down to essentials after all.

'Even the prisoners have bikes,' she reflected, as the sounds of laughter reached them from the bothy next door.

'They have that,' her man agreed. 'But then, *they* didn't have to pay for them.'

*　　　　*　　　　*

Kirsty and Meg had already perched themselves up in the dyke. On the lookout for the grocer's van. And Elspeth had begun to make her way down the hill from Achullen. Poised uncertainly on her doorstep, the young woman decided to join the other wives before Elspeth reached them. She found it easier to stand quiet, within the silence that Elspeth's presence always brought with it now, than to go crashing through, and into the middle of it.

Strange how herself and Elspeth, who had always had so much to speak about, now seemed to communicate through the voices of Meg and Kirsty.

'Grocer. *Quando?*' Luigi's voice rang across from the steps of the bothy. '*Quando?* Grocer.' Unwilling to respond, the young woman squeezed herself further into the circle of her silent neighbours.

'Your Italian friend is crying on you,' Kirsty nudged her, breaking the silence, turning away to confide in Elspeth. 'Little did I think. Little did I dream that a day would come, when we'd have to share the grocer's van with prisoners-of-war.'

'Italians at that,' Elspeth said. For *their* men, she concluded, *their* prisoners-of-war in Germany wouldn't get such liberties. *Their* men wouldn't have a copper in their pockets to lash out on anything they fancied.

'It's only pocket money,' the young woman protested. 'Only for little extras. Shaving soap. Things like that.'

'Shaving soap!' The very idea of it, Kirsty claimed, took her breath away. Though it seemed to leave her with enough breath to belittle the commodity, claiming that a bit of carbolic, 'worked up into a lather', was good enough for *her* man. An ounce of bogie a week. A pint of ale on a Saturday. That was the extent of Kirsty's man's 'extras'.

There was, the young woman thought, something in Kirsty's condemnation. *Her* man had said the self-same thing about the second-hand bikes. Extras were rare in their own lives, hard to come by.

'*Quando? Quando* come grocer?'

'For the love of goodness,' Meg advised the young woman, 'have a word with that Italian of yours, or he'll stand bawling there all night.'

69

'*Pronto!*' she shouted across to Luigi. 'Grocer *pronto*.' The anger she heard rising up in her voice was inexplicably directed against him.

'She can even *speak* Italian now,' Elspeth said, turning to the other wives.

✻   ✻   ✻

They rightly referred to the grocer's van, rather than to the grocer himself. Peering down on them from between its shelves, his bulk prevented them from having a real good look at his wares, as if he, himself, were reluctant to reveal them. What was it that 'the Eyetie' wanted, he demanded, in a tone that implied whatever it was, he might not be of a mind to supply it.

'Pig. Pig me like. *Prego*.'

Flummoxed by Luigi's request, the grocer's van threw it to the waiting wives for their consideration. ' "Pig," he says. Well, well then, so he would like pig.'

'It's bacon he wants.' The young woman stepped forward. '*Bacon*. That's what he wants.'

He would need coupons for that, the grocer's van snapped. And as far as *he* knew, prisoners didn't have coupons.

That was right, the young woman conceded. Their coupons were held in the camp. He could, she offered, have some of hers, since there was no law against that! There was no virtue in her offer.

70

It was just that bacon—a luxury at *any* time—was seldom on her own list.

Herself and Meg, Kirsty offered, would see Elspeth up the length of the hill. For it was just the night for a walk. It was, the young woman remembered, watching them set off together, the kind of night she liked in the days when she accompanied Elspeth. The frost sealed the world to itself. It held the earth, as the moon took to the sky. It would already have begun to weave its fine silver webs on every whin bush from here up to Achullen. She could never resist drawing her fingers through those fine silver webs. A compulsion for touch's sake. To see if they felt as cold as they looked. Strange that she should remember such a small pleasure with such regret.

'You no walk? No walk with friends?' Luigi put his arm across her shoulder.

'No. Too cold for me. Too much cold.'

       ✳   ✳   ✳

'Sileence!' Luigi shot up his arm in command, when she opened the door of the bothy. 'Sileence. Umberto write. *Lettera* for me. *Mama Mia.*'

Paolo, on his stool by the fire, sat entwining his rosary beads around his fingers. The way that Elspeth used to wind her wool on winter nights. '*Scusi,*' Paolo greeted her, starting to rise up from the stool. 'No, Paolo,' easing him down, she shook her head. 'YOU *scusi*. You *scusi* ME.'

71

Luigi, crouched over Umberto's shoulder, as if such close physical contact could instill Umberto with words, the words that Luigi himself struggled to find, was beginning to batter against the barrier of Umberto's objections and rejections.

It wasn't possible, Umberto insisted. 'Imposseeble' for Luigi to mention in a letter that some friends from Napoli had arrived at the main camp. Censorship, Umberto pointed out, would never pass that. Censorship, it appeared, would never pass any of the things Luigi wanted to write.

'*Perche? Perche? Perche* imposseeble? *PERCHE?*'

Perche. Luigi's anguished whys began to pervade the bothy, countered by the calm, sharp logic of the ex-schoolteacher, until it seemed that nothing worth communicating could ever be penned.

Tearing the letter from Umberto's hands, to utter the half-truths it contained—Health good . . . plenty rain . . . time soon pass . . . food OK . . .

'*Clock*,' she said, minding on her mission and moving towards the mantelpiece to reset their alarm clock. 'Tomorrow, one hour early. Tomorrow, winter come.'

✻   ✻   ✻

A cold snap had set in. On a morning like this, you'd want to crack the frost-bound world wide open. The men were already setting out to do so. Armed with forks to crash through the ice on the cattle troughs. The others armed with billhooks on their way to the turnip field, on an even more arctic expedition.

'It's neeps or forks,' Finlay was bawling at Luigi. It was always the same when the men were divided into two squads. It always set Luigi dithering, wondering which job would be the easier. Even now with the bogies starting to move off, he darted between one and the other, holding everything and everybody up.

'The one's as bad as the other,' Finlay roared. 'You can either break your back pulling neeps. Or dislocate your shoulder cracking ice. And I don't give a bugger *what* you do, so long as you get a move on and *do* it!'

'Gloves no good,' the young woman tried to persuade Luigi, as he hunched himself round to the back of the turnip bogie. Muffled from head to foot in his balaclava and top coat. Looking for all the world like a picture she had once seen of Scott of the Antarctic. A different kind of explorer, Luigi, but still an explorer adrift in an alien world of turnip shaws and cattle troughs.

'Gloves no good for turnips,' she assured him. 'Gloves get wet. Fingers get frozen.'

> *'O come all ye faithful*
> *Joyful and triumphant . . .'*

she could hear Kirsty carolling more clearly than

she could see her. A dim figure, sweeping her doorstep against the snow whirling down around her. A waste of energy, but not of spirit. Simply a bursting free from the ice-bound days.

'Thank God the snow's come at last!' Kirsty shouted across to her. 'It'll take the bite out of the air.'

Even so, Kirsty's largesse of spirit didn't extend to accepting the young woman's invitation to accompany her to Achullen Wood, in search of holly. Although there were holly trees in Achullen Wood, not a one of them, Kirsty claimed, had ever borne a berry. Not in all her years of knowing them.

But then, they were wary, Kirsty and Meg, of the wild abundance that flourished outside their own small, cultivated yards. And the wildness had long since gone out of the flowers they grew and cherished. Flowers with heart-remembered names. Snow in Summer. Lad's Love. Dusty Miller. Heart's Ease.

How horrified Kirsty had been last spring when the young woman had gathered hawthorn blossom and set it in a jar on her windowsill. Kirsty's mother would never allow her to bring hawthorn blossoms into the house, certain that trouble or death would follow in its wake.

She hadn't believed that of course. But the idea of it had darkened the white cloud of flowers, had dulled her pleasure in them. Sown by a word, superstition's omen became accepted.

Achullen Wood stood white and sculptured in

the precision of its winter, defying an intruder to leave a footmark that would break into the delicately traced signatures of its own inhabitants. Defying an intruder to sound out against its silence, the snap of the holly branches shouting sacrilege in her ears.

She had warned her well, Kirsty said, staring on the berryless bounty the young woman had lugged back to the Cottar Row. For Kirsty knew fine there would be not a berry on the holly. It would, she pointed out regretfully, have been far better to have collected fir cones in the autumn, and painted them all over with yon silver stuff, the way that wife had shown them at the W.R.I. Still, Kirsty conceded, they'd had more on their minds than silver cones in the autumn. Forbye, it was a real 'scutter' of a job. If you hadn't 'got the hands' for it. But surely, surely, the young woman wasn't going to kirn up her kitchen with that berryless stuff.

It was really for the Italians, the young woman explained. They set such store by Christmas.

It was to be *hoped*, Kirsty protested, that they wouldn't be kicking up a din, like they always did, with the comings and goings from the camp of strange Italians that you'd never set eyes on. And all the singing that was on them all, into all hours of the night.

✳ ✳ ✳

She had set the holly in a jar on the windowsill of the bothy. Three Christmas cards on their mantelpiece. And put the box of dates she had wheedled from the grocer's van on the table.

'*Buona Natale*,' she greeted the Italians. '*Buona Natale*.'

The singing that had rung out from the bothy last night left no echo behind itself this morning. If I could paint, she thought, staring round the bothy, I couldn't capture Christmas. Only a jumbled image of letterless days. Selected by time. Pounced upon. Held high in time's hands for microscopic examination.

'*Buona Natale*,' she said again to the silent figures on the frieze of her perception. '*Buona Natale*.'

'Christmas ITALIA!' mumbled Luigi from beneath the blankets.

'*Natale* here too, Luigi.'

'*ITALIA Natale*.'

'*Natale* everywhere.'

'*Prego. Molto gentile*.' Paolo's voice reached her as she made for the door. '*Grazie*.'

Maybe Christmas *could* only happen in Italy, she thought, gazing across on the turnip field where the men were already at work. There was no sign of it on the farm.

*   *   *

'We're in for it now, then,' her man prophesied, as

the bicycles rang past their door. 'That'll be some of them over from the camp. We'll be in for a night of it.'

Maybe the Mass the Italians had attended in the morning had worked some Christmas wonder—beyond the power of holly, and three Christmas cards.

'We were *invited*,' she reminded her man. 'You too.' *She* could please herself. But not *him*. He would never, he claimed, understand a word they were saying.

She didn't understand many of the words either, but she could sometimes interpret the sound of them. . . .

*   *   *

The whole of Italia seemed to be crowded inside the bothy. The emotionalism of the relationship between the prisoners something beyond her ken. A physical embrace between men, something she had never seen before. They were sparing of loving words and gestures, the men on the farm. If ever she were to set eyes on Finlay clasping Beel in his arms she would have thought they had lost their wits in a world that had come to an end.

'*Buona Natale, signorina.*' One of the visiting Italians stepped forward to greet her.

'*Buona Natale,*' she responded, smiling because she knew she had got the accent right.

'*Parla italiano. Lei parla italiano.*' He swung round to inform the company. '*Allora! Lei parla . . .*'

His reaction overwhelmed her, forcing her into truth. '*Poco italiano. Poco poco . . .*'

'*Poco. Poco!*' They began to surround her. Grinning in appreciation. '*Bene. Bene.*'

'Dance me.' Elbowing his way through them, Luigi laid claim on her. 'Dance. Me.'

✳   ✳   ✳

'*Che bella cosa,*' he sang, his head thrown back, his eyes closed as they circled as if in a trance.

'*Che bella cosa,*' the others took up the song, serenading her within a circle of music.

'*Che bella cosa . . .*'

Never before had she felt so desirable. Knowing in that moment how Eve must have felt, waking up from the trance of her creation, to look into the dark, appreciative eyes of Adam.

Coyness, which until now, she hadn't known she possessed, took over. Brought to the surface by her awareness of Paolo's presence. Surely he would see her *now*, reflected in the admiration of other men's eyes.

Tomorrow, she would feel ashamed of her posturing, of her emphasis on her physical attributes. So blatantly displayed, an offering to Paolo.

✳   ✳   ✳

It could never be Paolo. She realised that, catching a glimpse of him, seated on the windowsill, absorbed in conversation with a friend from the camp, unaware of her existence, apart from the circle of celebration.

The dream that had so often kept her awake at night would have to be put by, laid away, maybe forgotten in time. The desert island her imagination had created for herself and Paolo, flora'd and fauna'd for their sole benefit and appreciation, that island would sink down and disappear into a sea for which she had not yet conjured up a name. That had distressed her: a dream, to be whole in substance, demanded perfection in the smallest of its parts.

'One time posseeble,' Luigi whispered, as he saw her to the door when the evening ended. 'One time posseeble jiggy-jig. For *Natale*.'

For the first time, for seconds as long as centuries, she hesitated, trapped within her thoughts. She would lie quiet at nights now, by the side of her man, bereft of the ecstasy of her wakeful dreams, bereft of the possibility of Paolo.

'No time possible,' she said at last. 'Maybe,' she heard herself promise, aware of the anticipation that had come over Luigi. She owed him that much for her hesitation. 'Maybe . . . some day. One day.'

✻   ✻   ✻

'That looks like the minister.' Kirsty stopped in her tracks to rap on the young woman's window. 'I could swear it's him, on one of his visitations.'

The sight of anybody, far down on the main road, always demanded their attention. Crusoe, catching his first glimpse of Man Friday. Sometimes, sometimes, the young woman had a great urge to cup her hands against her mouth and shout across the distance to any passer-by. 'Look up. I'm here. Look up. And give me identity.' Prisoners though the Italians were, they would one day be free of this isolation. She envied them that.

When she was a child, on her rare jaunts to the country, she had thought that the fields and woods and all of the land belonged to everybody. To each and all. Took the brown furrowed fields for granted, the way she accepted the wild hyacinths growing in the woods. She hadn't realised that every acre of that wide, childhood land belonged to an individual, was the property of. And, for that property, other men worked the miracle of a precise and patterned earth, ploughing it, dragging it, rolling it to change its patterns to green shining corn.

Even now, grown up, the illusion would return, when she walked down to the village and turned to look back on the uplands she had left behind, seeing it the way a townsman might see it. The tractor quiet in the distance, purring across the fields. Beel and Finlay forking the hay for cattle fodder. Picturesque men. Silhouetted against the rick, a leisurely image. Unhurried, seen from a distance.

She knew now, though, that such images not only deceived the eye, they cheated the mind, for the tractorman was no leisurely tin toy figure, but a man who whiles needed the precision of a mathematician, or a lifetime's experience, to manoeuvre his machine through its different tasks and different gradients.

Screwing her eyes tightly together, she could see that the corn had already begun to bree, covering the fields with a fine green mist. Hard to believe that such fragility had survived the heavy roller that had gone over it yesterday, hard to believe it survived such an onslaught in its small, shimmering, elasticity.

✳   ✳   ✳

'Lift up sacks. Lift up tatties. Lift up shit.' Luigi grumbled as he came towards them at the end of a day spent in carrying sacks of potatoes to the lorry, for sale in the town. He hadn't yet learned that the only way to carry a heavy sack was to hoist it high on his shoulders. His inability to do so had not only irritated the men who knew how, but had impeded their own bent and burdened approach to the lorry, and had aroused Finlay's anger.

'Finlay speak me lazy,' he mourned. '*Everybody* speak me lazy. Plenty work me, Napoli. Plenty work . . .'

81

'Plenty skive here,' Kirsty muttered. 'You're not in Napoli now.'

Strange to hear the sound of Luigi's city echoed by Kirsty. As if Napoli was a place with which she was familiar, and one that was not up to much in her opinion. Kirsty had no intimacy with cities. Even the knowledge of her market town was proscribed to High Street, MacInley's Tearoom, and the bus terminal. For the young woman—with half her childhood spent in the streets—Luigi's Napoli merged easily into her own remembrance. Not even ignorance of its language could have made of her an exile from *Sturm und Drang*. Thrust and parry. Pitting of wits. And sleight of hand. . . .

'I believe him,' she said. 'Nobody's lazy when they're doing the thing they like to do.'

'*You* didn't like the threshing mill,' Kirsty pointed out. 'You said that *yourself*. On and on about it for days, but *you* did it. That's the difference. You *did* it.'

'Milk!' Luigi shouted from the door of the bothy. 'Milk for supper, me.'

'You'd better see to that one's milk,' Kirsty advised, turning to go. 'Or he'll stand bawling there all night. And *you*,' she reminded Luigi, in the passing, 'you had to wait till you was *born*.'

'Luigi can wait,' the young woman decided, catching up with Kirsty. 'He can just wait till the other Italians come.'

Time, since the Italians' Christmas party, had

taken on a quality of nightmare in the young woman's mind, had turned into a game of hide-and-seek, where the cry of 'I spy' became translated, on Luigi's tongue, to the persistent reminder, 'You promise. One day. You promise . . .'

Sometimes, the young woman remembered, sometimes in the lost days of childhood, the hiding place could become more fearful than discovery itself. She had felt safer when Paolo haunted her waking dreams than she felt now, confronted by the full-blooded reality of Luigi.

'I would have thought he would have keepit to the hill,' Kirsty said when the shepherd swung down into view. 'Lambing being just on top of him,' she concluded, straddling the seasons.

✳   ✳   ✳

A man apart, the shepherd. Solitary, working only with other men at the shearing and dipping, even his cottage was outdistanced from the Cottar Row. The young woman liked the shepherd, and the fine 'speaks' they had on their rare encounters. The things she had learned from them. Snow, warm enough to kill, if you sheltered within it and fell asleep in its warmth. Sheep that whiles got drunk, gorging themselves on the young broom. The broom was as potent as that when young and new. The ewe, with the mischance to fall on her back, that would be dead within the hour. The creature unable to raise herself up again, because she was not 'born balanced'. And hoodie crows, 'the carrion brutes', diving always to peck the eyes of the stillborn lambs.

She would like fine to work with the shepherd. There seemed to be no monotony to his days, unlike the other men, making their way home from the tattie shed. She had seldom seen them quicken their pace. They would walk in their downbent gait to their graves. It was monotony that was beginning to make herself feel old. Or maybe it was marriage that had shut a door, the door that led to romance and adventure, one that she had never given herself time to unlock.

'There's something amiss,' Kirsty said, as they watched the shepherd signalling to the men. 'Something gone wrong.'

'Combustion,' muttered Finlay, as he went past. 'Shepherd saw it steaming up as he happened by.' They'd gone, he roared in accusation to the men, and built the damned stack with stuff that was wersh. Too green. Too raw. And the best thing they could do now was to get themselves up to the barn for ladders, and move themselves down to the haystack.

Strange, the young woman thought, staring at the stack in the distance, standing as it had always stood. Nature secretly, stealthily, committing arson. Fire without flame.

There would be flame right enough, Kirsty assured her, if the stack was left to itself. They would soon see the flames rising when the men took the thatch from the top of the stack.

✳   ✳   ✳

Green and growing taller the corn now. Out now in the field the cattle nosed the grass, sniffing out their old smells again. The farm-workers pausing to catch their breath between the urgency of seasonal demand. 'Time now to straighten my back and light up my pipe,' as Beel expressed it. And he surely needed that, was Kirsty's dry observation, for she wondered why Beel ever bothered to smoke a pipe at all, since he never seemed to get the damned thing to draw.

But if the pace of the farm had slowed down, work in the cottages in the Row was beginning to speed up, was taking on frenzied proportions, Kirsty whitewashing the sills of her windows. And Meg, beating the life out of her 'clootie' rugs, gazing askance as the young woman swept past them, bound for Achullen Wood.

✳   ✳   ✳

'The weather,' Kirsty warned, 'could break any minute now.' The tattie planting would soon be on top of them, Meg reminded her. And by the looks of it, the summer would be gone before the young woman made a start to her spring-cleaning.

'The cleaning will keep,' she shouted back, when she had got beyond reach of their reproaches. 'The wild hyacinths won't.'

The mass of them cast a blue bloom across the wood itself. Forcing themselves up into the consciousness of the trees. The only wood flowers that had the power to impose such colour. The early snowdrops couldn't do that, she remembered, standing knee-high amongst the strong flowers. Nor the aconites. She had never been tempted to uproot the snowdrops, to take them away from the small, close intimacy of their groups. Meg and Kirsty always boasted that they loved flowers enough to let them grow. Maybe they had the right way of it. Maybe her love was too possessive. Too destructive.

Plunging her face down into their dew-drenched mass, her senses aching at the intensity of their scent . . .

> Shade-loving hyacinth
> Thou comest again
> And thy rich odour seems to swell the flow
> Of the lark's song
> The redbreast's lonely strain . . .

They *were* right, Kirsty and Meg. She had to admit that. For the wild hyacinths began to droop in her arms, limp from the moment she had uprooted them from the wood. Protesting as she did so with their broken, squelching cry.

'You go wood,' darting out of the bothy, Luigi looked accusingly down on the hyacinths. 'You no speak me you go wood. *Perche? Perche* you no speak wood? Me posseeble wood. You. You promise one day . . .'

All the water in the world could not revive the hyacinths. But she would never be guilty of such an offence against them again, for the wood had become proscribed territory. Luigi had unwittingly ensured that.

> *We'll go no more a-roving*
> *In the middle of the night*
> *Tho' the heart be ne'er so loving*
> *And the moon be ne'er so bright . . .*

*　　　　　*　　　　　*

'I'll never look a tattie in the face again,' Kirsty vowed, straightening herself up from the drill she was planting. It was enough to put you off tatties for life, Meg agreed, reminding them there was still the Kerr's Pinks to be planted yet. Her reminder causing them to stand in depressed contemplation of the work that still had to be done.

'What's all this then?' Beel shouted from his tractor. 'The Mothers' Meeting?'

'Fathers not invited.' The young woman's attempt at levity sounded flat to her own ears.

'You want to get your backside up off that

tractor,' Kirsty advised him, 'and get *your* back bent over the tattie drills.'

'No chance,' Beel laughed. 'I wouldn't want to do you all out of your jobs.'

'Cut the claik,' Finlay roared, taking a flying leap over the dyke, and landing himself amongst them in the tattie field. 'Just you keep your mind on your tractor,' he warned Beel. 'You're cutting the corners some fine. You'll have the whole bloody caboodle coupit in amongst the drills.'

It served Beel right, they agreed, as they stood uncertain whether to get on with their planting again, or to wait in hope of a full scale 'row' blowing up between Finlay and Beel, giving them a legitimate excuse for a breathing space. It was Kirsty who came to the conclusion that they would be well advised to get on with the planting. 'With Finlay in a mood like that. It's well seen that he'd got out of bed wrong side this morning.'

'Where to hell are the Italians?' Finlay demanded. 'I gave orders for every man jack of you to be at the tatties.'

The Italians, Beel reminded Finlay, were across there in the Nether Park, gathering stones and rooting up thistles as Finlay himself had ordered them.

'*Christ!*' Finlay's expletive brought Beel's tractor to a bumping halt, and riveted all attention on the field where the Italians were working. 'You've gone,' he accused Beel, 'you've gone and given the buggers billhooks. They'll have the legs cut off beneath each other.'

'Want to see the Italians come at the double?' the young woman whispered to Kirsty. 'Watch this, then.' Running to the dyke, she shouted across to the Nether Park, '*Bull*. Quick. *Run* Luigi. Bull come. Bull come quick.'

'You stupid-looking bitch,' Finlay thundered, as the Italians sent the billhooks flying and scrambled over the dyke to safety. 'You'll try that trick once too often.'

Lacking in appreciation. That was Finlay's trouble. The young woman felt resentful. At least she had managed to get the Italians on to the tattie field 'at the double'.

'You would think,' Kirsty commented, 'that the Italians would know the difference between a bull and a cow by this time.'

'It's all that tits,' Beel informed her, doubling up with laughter over his steering wheel. 'That's what gets the Italians muddled up. All that tits.'

It was Beel's 'pea-sized brain' that got Beel 'all muddled up', Finlay snapped, and the sooner he took himself out of Finlay's sight, the better.

*　　　*　　　*

The bad start to the morning set the 'mood' of the tattie planters for the rest of the day. The squad spirit had gone, with the Italians huddling dourly

89

together and Finlay and Beel stumping around the field, ignoring each other.

The young woman would never, not if she lived to be a hundred, get used to the sudden changes of mood that could come over the workers. You would think a field too wide for offence to close over it. The sky too high for offence to thrive beneath it.

The mood was infectious though. It was beginning to affect herself. She would never, she vowed, as she stumbled over the clods lying unbroken in the drill, she would never sing, laugh, dance, or try to cheer them up again.

Time itself began to be measured out in inches. Distance defined by the planting of a potato. Twelve inches one foot. One foot. One potato.

'Another rotten tattie,' Kirsty shouted over to Finlay, straightening herself up to wonder who on earth had he gotten to 'sort this lot out. Enough to put you clean off your supper,' she confided to the young woman since Finlay had taken no notice of her complaint. The young woman ignored it also. . . . 'I have piped unto you. And you have not danced. I have mourned with you. And you have not wept.' She would do neither. Never again, renewing her vow as she hopped over to the dyke to free her wellingtons from the clods that encrusted them. No wonder the townsfolk nicknamed them clod-hoppers. No amount of harrowing, rolling, raking or gathering would ever free their earth of fast-cleaving clods. . . .

'I'm just helping myself to a two three wee tatties for my hennies,' Kirsty was confessing to Finlay. 'Is that all right with you?'

'You can help yourself to the whole bloody field,' Finlay barked, loping past them to guide Beel and the tractor through the narrow field. Desperate now for one civil word out of anybody at all in the whole wide world, Kirsty turned to the young woman as a last resort. 'What about *your* hens? Are you not taking back a tattie or two for *your* hens?'

'*My* hens,' the young woman informed her, as she swayed to find her balance after a day rocking around in the tattie drills, '*my* hens wouldn't look at rotten tatties.'

✳   ✳   ✳

She was daft, they assured the young woman, as they stood waiting for the butcher's van. For they concluded that the hen she was holding preparatory to barter was 'worth a damned sight more than anything the butcher would give her in exchange'.

That wasn't important, it was just that the young woman couldn't face the thought of eating a hen that she had become acquainted with, had reared from a chicken. The farmer's wife, she pointed out, with all that sheep and pigs and cattle she owned, would never have thought of eating the creatures. There was no difference, in *that* respect, between herself and the farmer's wife.

There was, Kirsty insisted, all the difference in the world. 'The law' didn't allow the farmer to kill his own beasts. *Hens* were a different thing. You could please yourself what you did with your own hens. You had the choice. 'And that hen,' Kirsty concluded, eyeing it regretfully, 'would have made a fine pot of cock-a-leekie broth, enough to last two days.'

'And second day's broth's aye best,' Postie sang out, as she creaked past them on her bicycle towards the hill.

'You've got a letter for Elspeth then?' Meg ventured to ask.

'Official,' Postie said, in her postwoman's voice. 'Official.'

She never did give much away, did Postie, but, as Meg assured them, they would know the 'news' soon enough, when Elspeth made her way down to the van.

'No sign of that butcher yet?' Kirsty's man shouted from the tractor shed. The only thing the men folk could think of was their bellies, Kirsty snorted, ignoring her man's query. For Kirsty and Meg disliked weekends. It upset their routine, with the bairns out of school, in and out amongst their feet all the time. *She* should consider herself lucky, Kirsty turned in attack now on the young woman, what with her man being a cattleman, with no weekends off, and no bairns to drag around her tail all the time.

It depended, of course, on what Kirsty meant by 'luck'. That time, the young woman remembered, that time when the sick and squeamishness wouldn't leave her, and she had gone to the doctor. Pregnant he thought, insisting that she return with a sample of urine. She couldn't be pregnant, she had insisted, rejecting both his diagnosis and his sample bottle. Why not, he had demanded. Pointing out that she was young, strong and married. Because. She had tried to explain it to him. . . . Because. . . . You must *know*. When something important like that is happening. You must know. You must feel something. I never feel anything. That, he had assured her, was by no means uncommon. But it should be. She remained convinced of that, not to feel anything should be the most uncommon thing ever.

Did Kirsty or Meg know, or feel? She had never been able to ask them. If Elspeth had been married, and if Elspeth and herself were still friends, she might have asked Elspeth.

> *'Down in the valley*
> *Where nobody knows*
> *Stands a young lady*
> *Without any clothes'*

The bairns, circling around in front of the Row, giggled themselves to a standstill. 'God alone knows where the bairns pick up dirt like that,' Meg said.

At the school, Kirsty thought. Where else, she demanded. They themselves had learned more than lessons, after they went to school.

> *'She sang and she sang*
> *And she sang so sweet*
> *She sang Alick Corbie*
> *Off his feet'*

'Keep your noise down,' Kirsty admonished, when they caught sight of Elspeth making her way down the hill, 'and run off and play yourselves somewhere else.'

✳   ✳   ✳

It was as if they suddenly needed both space and quietness to observe Elspeth's approach, to read from her lineaments, the contents of the letter marked 'official'. *Her* secret still. Her gait, stately, deliberate as always, revealing nothing. Even the men, pausing to watch, were aware of the dignity with which Elspeth surrounded herself, although it proved no armour against the crude familiarities they voiced behind her back. 'I wouldn't touch Elspeth with *your* cock,' Beel boasted, laughing to Kirsty's man.

'*You'll* never get that chance,' the young woman assured them, quick with contempt. 'Elspeth happens to be particular.'

'I'm sorry, Elspeth,' Kirsty was saying.

'Me too,' Meg echoed.

'And me, Elspeth.' Compelled into utterance, the young woman spoke, knowing her words would be received in silence. 'I am sorry too.'

For it was, as Postie had described it, 'official'. Elspeth's Callum, no longer missing, had been discovered, identified and dead. A confirmation leaving no loophole for hope. All their condolences combined seemed to bring no consolation. Had it been some calamity that had befallen *themselves* now or in the past, they could have keened together in lament. But their men were safe, in reserved occupations. The realisation made the young woman feel uncomfortable, as if their immunisation might be offensive to Elspeth.

'I'm the King of the Castle'

Kirsty's small son declaimed from his stance on top of the dyke,

'Get down you dirty rascal.'

'Don't you *dare*,' his mother warned him, 'don't you dare *jump*.' He would go head-first into the ditch if he did, Meg remarked objectively, 'good trousers and all'.

'Jamie has found a puddock,' the small girls screamed, as they scrambled up out of the ditch, their coloured knickers bobbing up amongst the bracken like wild convolvulus flowers. 'He's found a puddock. He's away for a reed to blow it up.'

Swerving to catch him as he rushed past her, the young woman grabbed Jamie by the shoulders, shaking him to a standstill. 'If you blow up that puddock,' she warned him, 'I'll *kill* you.'

Gathering up the small frog that sat stunned at her feet, she carried it back to the bank and set it down amongst the bracken. The force of her anger surprised herself, as she stood waiting for the trembling that had come over her to die down. It, she realised, had been no idle threat, but uttered in a moment when she felt capable of, and inclined to, murder.

'I was just saying to Meg,' Kirsty informed her when she rejoined them, 'I was just saying we never go down to the rocks to gather winkles now.'

'We always used to,' Meg remembered, 'when the tide went out.'

They had spoken. The young woman had the feeling that they might never utter again. Elspeth never would. She accepted that. But at least she would not have to walk in perpetual silence through the high places of this upland country.

✳   ✳   ✳

It was not until Elspeth had gone, that they got down to the heart of the matter. There would be neither widow nor war pension for Elspeth, her not being married, like. You had to be legally married to get a widow's pension, or badly wounded to get a war pension.

Still, they concluded, having pondered it over, it could have been worse. Elspeth could have been left with fatherless bairns to bring up. Though that would have been unlikely in *her* case, for she was well into her forties was Elspeth, and bound to be 'past it' by now. Come to think of it, when you really got down to it, if it had been one of *their* men that had been killed in the war, their loss would have been far greater than Elspeth's. That stood to reason. . . .

Dear God *forgive* me. The young woman was appalled by the thought that had sprung so sudden and unbidden into her mind. If her man had gone to the war and been killed, she would have had a second chance. Another time to start a new life, to be up and away from the ingrowing, incestuous way of the farm, in search of something that had eluded her. Often, in the evenings, when she stood watching the flow of traffic far down on the main road and the smoke rising up from trains rushing past on the other side of the firth, it seemed as if a whole vista of escape unfolded itself before her eyes. . . .

So many roads lead outwards
There's one that leads to London
And one that leads to Rome
Some lead to the mountains
Others to the plain
But every road that's taken
Must lead you back again

Dear God. Forgive me. . . . Forgiveness, though, she had discovered from the Italians, was never automatically granted, but paid for by penance, which she attempted now, dedicating this fine spring day to dirt, scouring her kitchen from top to bottom.

'My! But you've been hard at it the day.' Her man's appreciation of the bright kitchen moved her by its innocence. Sometimes, now and again, she would have liked to have been blind, so that the small externals that always seemed to surround him could never disarm her—hacked hands, threadbare shirts.

'You've cut yourself with the neep hasher,' she said, covering his hand with her own. Her frock, she remembered, was almost paid up, in Kirsty's catalogue. She could put a new order in now. 'A couple of working shirts,' she suggested, as they sat down to their supper. 'You're in need of them.'

'What about *you*. Is there nothing you're needing for yourself?'

'Nothing,' she assured him, 'I'm fine.' The truth of her statement took herself by surprise.

Meg had 'gone clean off Kirsty'. The young woman now found herself in the circumference of their triangle. 'A certain party', according to Meg, had 'let the cat out of the bag'.

'*A certain party*', always unidentified, always malevolent, who drifted invisible in and out of the perimeter of cottar life, causing havoc whenever she appeared, intrigued the young woman. This time, the nameless one threatened to disrupt the old order of turnip hoeing.

According to Meg, Kirsty and her family had decided to take on piece-work at the hoeing this year. And you knew what piece-work was, paid by the length of the work done. Couldn't you just see Kirsty and her brood taking down the neep drills like the hammers of hell. Anything for an extra bob or two. Leaving them, the ordinary workers, all behind like cows' tails. And paid by the hour. Showing *them* up. That, Meg emphasised, was what 'got her goat, a showing up'. She didn't, she assured the young woman, mind the fat wage packets that Kirsty and her family would collect, for, strictly between herself and the young woman, Kirsty needed every extra penny she could get, to keep up with the payments on all the stuff she was forever ordering out of that catalogue of hers.

There might, the young woman suggested, be no need of piece-work, now that they'd got the

Italians. 'The Italians', Meg reminded her, made a right soss-up of thinning the kale. Riving everything that grew right up out of the drills, driving Finlay demented. God help the crop if the Italians were let loose with the hoe, amongst small finnicky things like young neeps. But the young woman, Meg conceded, pausing in her tirade, to make the allowance, the young woman could please herself about taking on the hoeing. As for Meg, she was by no means sure if she 'would be in the mind to put in an appearance' at the turnip field.

The soil was in fine tilth for hoeing, softened by last night's rain, so that everybody on the farm—including Meg—had turned up to get the hoeing over and done with, while earth and weather were in such fine fettle. Even Else, the servant girl from the farm, had joined them in their task.

Meg was right. Hoeing was proving competitive. The blisters were already beginning to rise on the young woman's hands. Tomorrow, Meg pointed out, the blisters would break and then the *real* agony would begin. But by the end of the week, her hands would become as hard as the handle of the hoe itself. She just wasn't holding her hoe at the right slant, Meg said, holding out her own unblistered hands for inspection.

Times like these, the young woman felt imprisoned within the circumference of a field. Trapped by the monotony of work that wearied the body and dulled the mind. Rome had been taken. The

Allies had landed in Normandy, she'd heard that on the wireless. 'News' that had caused great excitement in the bothy, crowded with friends, gesticulating in wild debate. Loud voices in dispute. Names falling casually from their tongues, out of books from her school-room days. The Alban Hills. The Tibrus . . . 'O Tibrus. Father Tibrus. To whom the Romans pray . . .' Even in her schooldays, those names had sounded unreal. Outdistanced by centuries, from another time. Another place. The workers in the fields made no mention of such happenings. All their urgency was concentrated on reaching the end riggs at the top of the field. The long line of army jeeps roaring down along the main road provided nothing more than a moment for straightening their backs, never impinging on the consciousness of the turnip field.

'*Che?*'. . . tugging at her shoulder, Luigi gesticulated towards Else. '*Ragazza . . . Che?*'

'Servant,' she told him. 'Works for boss's wife.'

'*Bella . . . Bella ragazza . . .*' She could hear Luigi shouting. She could have misheard of course, she was so used to Luigi applying the words to herself.

'She's a daft bitch, *that.*' Meg drew their attention to Else, as they stopped for a moment, before starting up on a new rigg. 'Skirling round the field there, with that Italian panting at her tails.' It was easily seen that Finlay wasn't around. He'd soon put the clampers down on a carry-on like that.

'You're supposed to start a new rigg when you're

done with the old one,' Kirsty shouted in warning to Luigi, 'so you'd better get a move on.'

'*Non capisco* me,' Luigi grinned as Else dodged giggling past them. 'Me no understand.'

'Me no understand,' Kirsty mimicked, turning aside to the others. 'He can understand fine when there's a bit of skirt around. And that Else is just as bad,' she concluded. 'Anything in trousers.'

✴   ✴   ✴

Ragazza. Ragazza. The words stuck in her mind, and depressed the young woman as they made their way home from the turnip field. *Ragazza.* A title to which she felt she was losing her claim.

She hadn't got much to say for herself tonight, Kirsty commented. If it was the blisters on her hands that was bothering her, she would get used to that, all she had to do was to steep them in water as hot as she could thole, with a good fistful of coarse salt thrown in. It would nip right enough, Kirsty assured her, but, by faith you, it would fairly harden up the skin on her hands.

It was jealousy that ailed the young woman. Not of Else, herself, but of the single freedom Else enjoyed. Older than the young woman, Else was still '*ragazza*'.

I'm here for ever, she thought, staring round the dim kitchen, before bracing herself to tackle its demands.

The bourtrees, in full blossom, arched themselves across the track that led to the main road, breaking up the vista of the world beyond the farm. The young woman could no longer nip round the side of the house to gaze on the traffic far down the road, could no longer imagine that time when she would slip quiet down the track into the wide world. She had always imagined that moment, but had kept postponing it. . . . Tomorrow. Next Friday. This time next week. Still holding on to its bright secret possibility. Some day. One day. . . .

> *With the bright pennies cold on my eyes*
> *I shall fly up to the warm sun*
> *And leave my shift where it lies . . .*

The bairns had already plundered the blossoms of the bourtrees, leaving them strewn across the track, froths of cream-coloured lace. Soon their berries would hang down in long purple chaplets, safe from the bairns. Warned off by their mothers' cries of 'poison!'. Or near enough safe, for danger itself was a compulsion to taste. And bitter to the tongue. Eyeing each other with apprehension, in anticipation of one or other, or all, dropping dead on the spot.

She came upon them congregated round the Italians, squatting on the steps of the bothy, shirtless in the sun. Their attention concentrated on the toy bogie which Paolo was hammering out for Kirsty's son.

> *'Who's the lucky boy*
> *That's going your way'*

the singer on the wireless enquired through the open windows, to send the young woman waltzing down the length of the Cottar Row in accompaniment.

> *'To kiss you good night*
> *In the doorway?'*

'Finlay wouldn't like *that*,' Kirsty proclaimed, bursting out from her hens' ree, and breaking up both the solo performance and the carefree mood of the sunlit day, commanding their attention to Beel's tractor, which stood facing up to Achullen. That tractor, she informed them, would never start off first go—not facing up the hill like that. Still, she admitted, before disappearing back into the hens' ree, that was *Beel's* concern, and she, Kirsty, 'washed her hands of the whole affair'.

　　　*　　　　　*　　　　　*

Kirsty's knowledge of the tractor, and of the demerits of Beel who worked it, always impressed the young woman. She always seemed to know when Beel had 'cleaned' the plugs, and, even more frequently, when he had 'forgotten' to clean them.

'It was just,' Meg said, sidling across from her doorstep to confide in the young woman, it was

104

just that Kirsty's man was fed to the back teeth working the old Davy Brown tractor, and was ettling to get his hands on Beel's International. That, Meg concluded, was all there was to it.

Who was of a mind to go for firewood then, Finlay, stumping round the corner, demanded to know. For although it was still summer, they were already getting ready for winter, all set to cut down the old trees for cottars' firewood.

They could all freeze to death if they liked then, Finlay threatened, confronted by their lack of response, but, by God, he vowed, if he were to set eyes on a one of them, crawling round the steading in search of paling posts when winter did come . . . There was nothing, he informed them, that he himself liked better on a winter's night, than just to fling a leg up on each side of the mantelpiece, and spit into a good roaring fire. But it was up to them, he admitted, for Finlay realised that the cutting down of old trees was voluntary. Free firewood for those who took the trouble to cut it down for themselves.

'Wood. Come wood. Today posseeble.' The young woman turned to find Luigi at her shoulder. 'You promise. You promise one day. Today. Posseeble.'

For the first time, for a long time, armoured by truth, she could look Luigi in the face. 'Today no possible. No possible wood. Me byre. Cows. Milk.'

'No posseeble. No posseeble. *Sempre* no posseeble, no posseeble, no posseeble, NO POSSEEBLE . . .'

The anger rising in Luigi's voice had reached the others, quiet and speculative, as, turning on his heel, Luigi rejoined them at the bothy door.

'What's *she* seeking now?' Meg broke through the silence as Else, like some runner from a battle-field crashed in amongst them. Their relationship with the farmer's wife's servant was cautious. Wary. Something in domestic service seemed to eat up character, to form the spy, the gossip, the snob and the hypocrite, seeing always the underside of their employers' lives. Sometimes though, on occasions like this, Else had her uses, warning them now that 'the mistress is on the road. Collecting for the foreign missions, making her way up to the shepherd's house at this very minute.'

There was no call to warn *her*, Kirsty claimed. The Queen herself, if so be she'd a mind, was welcome to come into Kirsty's house without warning. Not so, the young woman. The sun had infiltered itself between her and her morning chores, and the farmer's wife would be more interested in the state of her husband's cottar house, than in far-flung foreign missions.

'Wood,' Luigi was urging Else. 'Everybody go wood. *You* like? You like go wood?'

He had no need to take that one the length of the wood, Meg observed, as they watched the giggling tug-of-war that waged in front of them. No need to go further than the barn door with that one. That, Meg impressed on her avid listeners, was why the last servant was sent packing. Bag and baggage down the road. It was Meg's own man that had 'catched them at it'. With a lorry driver. Up against the barn door. He'd gotten a right fleg, had Jamie. All he could see was big bare thighs. 'Disgusting, just.'

'Big bare thighs'. The image haunted the young woman, all the way to the byre. Usually she liked the byre. She was good at milking the cows. At ease and at one with the job in hand. Her face pressed against the cow's warm flank, sensing the intimacy between them. A need on the cow's part to give. And on her own to receive.

'Yield'—they used the right word for it, country folk. For although the cow could be serenaded, or talked into yielding her milk freely, she could never be forced. But the young woman was in no mood to apply such persuasion. 'Big bare thighs'. She should, she knew, share Kirsty's disgust at such an image, but found herself instead, resentful of Else, in envy of her.

'She's slow in letting her milk down.' Her man, puzzled, hovering by the side of the stall. 'She shouldn't be going dry yet. She's not that long calved. I'm saying . . .' His words lost impact within the vision of Luigi, squatting brown and shirtless in the sun. 'I'm saying she shouldn't be going dry yet.' The sharp and sudden outbursts of anger that had of late begun to possess her at inexplicable times, were threatening now. She recognised that by the trembling that had come over her body, by the word of accusation, fighting within her. Pounding to get out . . . 'It's not fair. You *had* your life. You had time. . . .'

The trembling was easing down now and she hadn't uttered. The relief of that poured out from her in a sweat that was cold, but set her on her normal course again. Grasping the cow's teats firmly within her hands, she drew them down, until the beat of milk falling into her pail kept rhythm with the song rising in her throat. . . .

> *Will you gang to Kelvin Grove*
> *Through its birches let us rove*
> *Will you gang to Kelvin Grove*
> *Bonnie lassie O . . .*

✳   ✳   ✳

If the wild hyacinths couldn't endure being plucked from their wood in full bloom, they might, the young woman thought, as she planted out the bulbs she had uprooted, accept and survive transfer to her own yard. That such tiny bulbs could produce such a profusion of blossom intrigued her. The improbable becoming possible. Their tiny comet tails curling round the bulbs, transforming legend into a truth. Sudden and clear, she remembered, the wild hyacinths were, she had learned at school, Persephone's favourite flower, and had followed her

108

deep and down and halfway to Hades. Hades. The word, shooting up out of memory, pleased her. She must, she thought, smiling, use it for the confusion of Kirsty. . . . It isn't hell, Kirsty. It's Hades, that's what the Greeks called it. . . .

'*Perche? PERCHE?*' Getting to her feet she confronted Luigi. '*Perche?* You no come bothy. *Perche?*'

'Because . . .' Answers in their multitudes swirled in her head, too elusive to be caught, to be worked in concrete. 'Because. Me busy. Work outside. Finish . . .' It wasn't explanation enough. She knew that by the rigid disbelief on Luigi's face. Turning away, she was unable to look on him in the clear light of day, for she had raped his privacy, had conjured up his every intimacy in fantasies covered by the night. She felt the shame of it, tangible, porous, oozing out to settle on her face.

'Come,' Luigi loosened his grip on her shoulder. 'Come. Speak bothy. One *minuto*. Paolo. Umberto gone camp. Come.'

※   ※   ※

The drought had settled itself down to stay. The cows, huddling together in splatches of shade under the trees, shifting as the shade shifted. The last of the summer's flowers drooping in the yards. The hot iron that was earth pinching away at their roots. Only the corn throve and rejoiced in the thick blanket of heat that had flung itself across the land,

109

but then corn always grew harsh and strong. With neither flower nor fragrance. For utility's sake. . . . 'If only the rain would come,' Kirsty lamented, 'it would wash away all the dust.' There seemed little sign of that. The mist was rising up across the firth, eliminating the sea itself. . . .

'Mist from the sea brings honey to the bee,' the young woman reminded her.

'You wouldn't think,' Kirsty commented, as the Italians drooped past them, 'that the heat would affect *them* like that, coming from a hot place like Italy.' At least, she remembered, they'd always had the manners to give you 'Fine morning' in passing. 'It must be this heat affecting them.'

It was neither the heat, nor lack of manners, that had set the seal of silence on the Italians. The young woman sensed that. It was a subtle change that had come over their relationship with herself, and with each other. She had sensed it since the day she had accepted Luigi's invitation to the bothy.

Her waking dreams of the night taking on confused dimensions. Her body that had taken her unaware, asserting a life of its own, clamouring for its needs, lay quiet now, cold with apprehension. While her mind whirred blind and bat-like, seeking for escape. Her thinking taking on a quality of nightmare. Naked. She would go into the bothy, offering herself to Paolo and Umberto. So that by this act of giving herself in bribery, they would feel no resentment. Sometimes, her thinking extended

110

to include all the friends of the Italians. She was sure that she had seen speculation in their eyes, and had heard the sound of knowingness in their salutations.

'You no speak. No speak Paolo. No speak Umberto,' she would urge Luigi, when the need for his reassurance overwhelmed her. 'No speak no person.'

'No speak me. Me no speak *persone*. *One* time. One more time. Posseeble. Me no speak.'

She would like to believe that, despite the hint of blackmail, she would like to believe it. Sometimes, times like now, she could will herself into belief. Standing safe, flanked between Kirsty and Meg, as if time itself had moments of compassion. Willing to turn back on itself and allow her a momentary illusion of security in familiar things. Although she was discovering familiar things could no longer be taken for granted, but commanded an absolute concentration on themselves. . . . 'That's that then. For another day. . . .' Even her man's nightly greeting, when he got in at night from the byre, although never varying and heard a hundred times, took on a new significance. Another day 'got through'. Brought without mishap to a satisfactory close. Ordinary things, enclosing her briefly within their own assurance.

'It's come round again,' Kirsty was saying, as they gazed down on the grain-ranked fields. For, it seemed to Kirsty, 'like yesterday, since we were at the stooking last year.'

'O it is but a week the morn'

The young woman sang. In sudden remembrance.

> *'Since I was weel and hairstin corn*
> *But something in my head gaed wrang . . .'*

An old song that, Meg said, older than themselves. A long time since they'd heard it. 'The Dying Ploughboy', Kirsty informed them, taking up the words herself.

> *Farewell my nags my bonnie pair*
> *For you I'll yoke and lowse nae mair*
> *Farewell my maister . . .*

God but they were in good voice the day, Finlay commented, on his way to the tractor shed. 'The Glasgow Orpheus Choir will have to look out for itself.'

At least, they consoled themselves, when Finlay had passed out of hearing, *they* didn't need 'The Barley Bree' to put *them* in good voice.

They should have said *that* to Finlay. An odd thing that, they agreed, contemplating its oddness. You always knew the right thing to say, when the chance to say it had gone.

❉ ❉ ❉

The binder had broken down. Now that the damned thing was at a standstill, Finlay informed the women, there was no need for them to stand around claiking. One of them, he suggested, might just take a turn up to Achullen, to see if Elspeth was of a mind to give a hand to the stooking. Now that they had lost the Italians. . . . Lost the Italians. The phrase took the young woman by surprise. The unexpected kindness of it. She would go, she volunteered. She was used to the climb. More than that, she needed to go. Needed to know that if Elspeth decided to work with them again, whether it could be if not in friendship, at least in tolerance. Not in a silence that would straddle itself across the seasons of their lives on the land.

It would have been easier to take the track through the heather, but she was not ready to take that track again. In years to come maybe, in another time, she might return to the place. But the climb released something within her self. Straightening up to stand high and knee-deep amongst the russet bracken crackling round her legs, the sun, it seemed, had never set with such fire and flame as it was setting now, a hill-crest fire, she remembered. Far beneath her the Cottar Row took on a new perspective, dwindling, huddling within the farm-steading, as if seeking for anonymity. Only yesterday, it had been the pivot around which the whole world revolved, before it had whirled and shuddered to a stop.

'No more corn. No more hayeerst. No more tatties,'
Luigi had proclaimed, as he rushed past her window, dodging the bikes of prisoners from the camp,
and shouting through the clamour of their bells.
'Tomorrow. Go home. Italia. Home Napoli.'

Again, the young woman had the feeling that the
whole of Italia was squeezed into the narrow length
and breadth of the Cottar Row, even Kirsty startled
by the sudden din, disapproving of the uninhibited
displays of emotion taking place in front of her eyes,
laughter and tears no longer rational, no longer
manifestations which separated joy from sorrow.
Even Kirsty was disarmed, as Luigi swept her off
her doorstep, whirling her along the length of the
Cottar Row. . . .

> *O are you sure the news is true*
> *And are you sure he's weel*
> *Come Jade put on your Sunday frock*
> *Good wife put by your wheel . . .*

Relief, in one great gush, was the young woman's
first reaction to the news. Like one who has been
granted a last minute reprieve. 'One time,' Luigi
was whispering. 'Today. One time. For last. . . .'
She would truly never know whether she had
yielded to the instinct of her body or to a sense

114

of long loss that the word 'last' had evoked within her. 'The dream', both the Bible of her childhood and those who read from it, had tried to din into her, 'the dream' could only come true 'through a multitude of busyness'. The 'busyness' was now all that remained. 'One last time,' she said to Luigi.

✳   ✳   ✳

They had taken separate tracks up through the heather, herself and Luigi, apprehension increasing as she watched him come towards her.

> *Come to the stolen water*
> *Come leap the guarded pale*
> *Come pluck the flower in season*
> *Before desire shall fail*

Her apprehension was justified. A subtle change had come over their relationship, as if their roles had been reversed.

The man who stood before her was no longer a prisoner. No longer a servant of circumstances, as she herself remained. Tomorrow he would be free to return to a world in which she would have neither part nor power. The triumph of this glistened on Luigi's face, glinted in his eyes, as he leant forward to embrace her. . . . 'Napoli. *Pronto*. Napoli.' The words, gasped in her ear, were not intended for her hearing, but words of affirmation. Of confirmation

115

for himself. She was aware of that, as he eased her down into the heather.

In her fantasies of the night, consummation had been a perfect thing, requiring no comment. Needing none of the reassurance she heard herself beseeching now. 'ME *amo*, Luigi? ME *amo* . . . ?'

'*Si, si. Ti amo.*'

'*Sempre*, Luigi. *Sempre.*'

'*Sempre. Si.*'

It was to the sky above that Luigi spoke, staring up at it as he lay, his hands clasped beneath his head. Staring as if Napoli itself was reflected within it. Raising herself slow and clumsy up from the heather, she had stood wondering how she could get her feet to carry herself, and the corpse of illusion within her, down from the hill with some small remnant of dignity.

*　　　　*　　　　*

The eyes of the workers gathered round Kirsty's door seemed to measure each step of her approach to the Cottar Row. The silence that had come over them when she turned the gate of her cottage, exploded the instant she reached them. Where had *she* been then, they demanded in chorus, as if she had forgone the privilege of being witness to great events.

For Else, taking the short cut through Achullen Wood, on her afternoon off, had been jumped on. Assaulted. Near enough ravished. If it hadn't been for Beel there, taking a turn through the wood. He'd heard the skirls of her in the nick of time. One of the Italians. Though which one, Beel wasn't rightly sure. For the man had taken to his heels, and Beel only got a glimpse of his back.

That could well be, they agreed, with all the Italians that were around the day. And the height they were at. Forbye, Kirsty's Alick remembered, Else was very thick with the Looeeshee one. They'd all noticed that. So thick, Kirsty remarked, that he'd have no need to ravish her.

It wasn't Luigi. It couldn't have been Luigi, the protest forced itself up in the young woman's mind, but stuck, somewhere down in her throat. What was more, Jeems reminded them, there was neither hair nor hide of the Looeeshee one. The other two Italians were in by the bothy, it seemed like there was nothing on *their* conscience.

Don't let Luigi come in sight. . . . The young woman's prayer rose up in panic. . . . Make him take the back way. Dear God, don't let them see him coming down the hill. . . .

If it was the Looeeshee one, Meg prophesied, there would be no Italy for him. No Napoli, that place he was always on about. As if it was the only place on the face of this earth.

It could have been any of the Italians, the young woman found her voice at last. There was a crowd of them here the day. They'd all know soon enough, Alick promised. According to Beel, they were taking

117

the prisoners back to the camp to interrogate them, Else and all, to identify. As for himself, Alick declared, there was no doubt in *his* mind. No doubt at all, for there was still no sign of the Loogee one. And that, surely, spoke for itself.

Only she could speak for Luigi. Something she felt compelled to do. But in the doing she was aware that her world as she now knew it would change, that the relationships she had begun to form would alter. She herself might survive the condemnation of the Cottar Row. It was the burden of shame within herself, and which would be extended to, and cast over her man, that was beyond enduring.

They could go away though, to another farm. They would easily get a job. They were good workers. A clean breast. A new start. The prospect beginning to light up in her mind, was snuffed out by the sudden remembrance of the Stand Still Order, that prevented farm-workers from leaving the land. There would be no other farm, no hiding place. No Roma. No Napoli.

So this was what it was like to be a prisoner. Small wonder that her attempts to console the Italians had been futile. Unable to interpret their language, which might have given more shape, more meaning to their experience.

Nothing for look. . . . She remembered in a sudden despairing survey of the landscape in front of her . . . In Scotland. Nothing for look. . . . She *knew* now, how it must have seemed to Luigi.

'It wasn't Luigi.' She heard herself telling the officer. 'It couldn't have been Luigi.'

. . . Father forgive me for I have sinned . . .

That, she realised, must be the easiest part of the confessional. The sinfulness announced, but the sin not yet defined. The officer's eyebrows rising up in perplexity, demanded definiton.

'Luigi was with me. Up in the heather. When . . . that happened to Else.'

'I see.' He didn't, not clearly. His hands scrabbled amongst the papers on his desk as if proof of her statement could be found there. Or maybe, maybe she thought, he was searching for words that could afford her a loophole.

'The time?' he asked. The precise time she had spent with Luigi, could she remember that?

'No.' She couldn't remember that. 'Not precisely.' Time out of bounds, time out of mind, time of that kind defied precision.

Her relationship with the Italian, was it of 'an intimate nature'? Yes, she had known the nature of the barrow-boy from the slums of Naples, had instantly recognised it, and had deeply understood it. But she knew that was not what the officer meant by 'intimacy'—knowing. Abraham and Sarah, she remembered, recalling long sermons in the kirk

119

of her girlhood, shortened by her avid researches through the Old Testament. Knowing and begetting.

'Yes,' she said to the officer.

'A prisoner and a civilian, *any* civilian,' the officer was emphasising, 'in such circumstances . . . You understand?' His words fading in horror of the realisation that engulfed her. The conviction against Luigi would stand, confirmed by *her* compulsive confession. Else, by admitting that she could not 'identify', had spared him that.

Twice she had lost the rudiments of dignity, that outward physical dignity that held the visible self together. Once in the heather with Luigi, and now on leaving the officer's room. Strange, that on both occasions it was the landscape, the land's life, against which she had protested strongly, that came to her temporary release, diminishing horror.

Losing herself in the absorption of the solitude of the dark mountain peaks on the other side of the water. Dissolving with herself in their indifference to pain, blame or shame.

*   *   *

'That's that then,' Finlay said as they straightened themselves up from the stooking to wave goodbye to the jeeps crammed with Italian prisoners on their way to home and freedom. 'The Looeeshee one will not see that Napoli of his in a hurry. Poor bugger.'

'Poor bugger right enough,' Beel agreed. 'For

120

there's damn all wrong with Else. A bit tousled and scrattit, but as right as rain now that she's gotten over her skirling and blubbering. Beginning to brag about it now. And no more ravished than Kirsty standing there was ravished.'

She herself, Kirsty admitted, had never had much time for the Looeeshee one. Too cocksure of himself. But for all that, knowing Else, no man body needed to go the length of rape with that one, not even Looeeshee.

That was as maybe, Finlay pointed out, grabbing the sheaves to set their minds, by his own example, back to the stooking again. 'One of you,' he suggested, 'might just take a turn up to Achullen to see if Elspeth's of a mind to give us a hand now that we've lost the Italians.'

✳   ✳   ✳

Elspeth, on her knees, was uprooting the withered nasturtium leaves that drooped amongst the white-washed stones around her door.

'Finlay says,' the young woman addressed Elspeth's back, rigid and bent, 'Finlay was wondering, Elspeth . . .'

'So. Finlay was wondering, was he?' Elspeth spoke without raising her eyes from the ground.

'Elspeth,' the young woman knelt by the bent figure, to make sure that Elspeth would hear. 'They've gone. The Italians. They've gone, Elspeth.'

'You was saying about Finlay?' Heaving herself to her feet Elspeth flung the withered nasturtium leaves over the fence, keeping a firm grip on the trowel in her hand, as if one wrong word would set it and herself down in attack among the stones again. 'Finlay. You was saying about Finlay . . .'

'The Italians, Elspeth, they've gone.'

'I see.' Elspeth stood considering what she saw. Her own pain or a reflection of pain that betrayed the young woman by rising sudden up out of its secrecy to look out of her eyes.

'You'd better come in.' Scraping her trowel careful and clean on the grindstone by the door, she repeated the invitation. 'You'd better come on inside.'

*　　　　　*　　　　　*

Only the empty bookshelves in Umberto's corner and the cigarette stubs lying in the grate remained as proof that the bothy had recently been inhabited. Staring around it, the young woman's eyes came to rest on the poster of the Madonna still hanging on the wall. Askew now, as if her usefulness was over. She'd had a hard time, this Scottish Madonna, miracles demanded daily, blame and praise in equal measure.

It was when she was turning to go that the young woman noticed the ship inside a bottle lying on the table. She had caught brief glimpses of it in

122

Paolo's furtive hands, but now it lay revealed in completion. Lifting it to examine it she saw the note hidden beneath it. . . .

Dina
Con amore e molta felicità
Paolo   Umberto   Luigi

They had never known her real name, she remembered. And had bequeathed her with a name of their own choice.

'Wifie', the general title of the Cottar Row touched both her mind and her mouth with irony. Wifie. Luigi would never have found the Italian word for that in his dictionary. Wifie, the title that had made her feel old before her time. Quine. Lass. That was different now, but used rarely, and only by the men.

'How did they get that ship into the bottle?' the bairns demanded, crowding round the bothy door. 'How did they get it inside?'

She didn't know either, it would remain a marvel and a mystery. But she knew what '*con amore*' meant, that was what she did know.

Also by Jessie Kesson, from B&W:

THE WHITE BIRD PASSES

Set in the back-streets of a Scottish city in the 1920s, *The White Bird Passes* is the unforgettable story of a young girl growing up in 'the Lane'. Poor, crowded and dirty—but full of life and excitement—the Lane is the only home Janie MacVean has ever known. It is a place where, despite everything, Janie is happy. But when the Cruelty Man arrives, bringing with him the threat of the dreaded 'home'—the orphanage that is every child's nightmare—Janie's contented childhood seems to be at an end.

Jessie Kesson's classic autobiographical novel is a gritty and moving portrayal of a young girl facing up to hardship and deprivation, written with warmth, humour and insight.

'Completely frank, transparently honest and deeply moving' COMPTON MACKENZIE

'Miss Kesson writes beautifully, her strong, delicate prose full of poetry and humour'
DAILY TELEGRAPH

'Beg, borrow or steal this book'
NORMAN MACCAIG

Available from all good bookshops, or direct from the publishers:

B&W Publishing,
233 Cowgate, Edinburgh,
EH1 1NQ.

Tel: 0131 220 5551